DAY
TRADING
OPTIONS

DAY TRADING OPTIONS

*Profiting from Price Distortions
in Very Brief Time Frames*

Jeff Augen

Vice President, Publisher: Tim Moore
Associate Publisher and Director of Marketing: Amy Neidlinger
Executive Editor: Jim Boyd
Editorial Assistant: Myesha Graham
Operations Manager: Gina Kanouse
Senior Marketing Manager: Julie Phifer
Publicity Manager: Laura Czaja
Assistant Marketing Manager: Megan Colvin
Cover Designer: Chuti Prasertsith
Managing Editor: Kristy Hart
Project Editor: Betsy Harris
Copy Editor: Cheri Clark
Proofreader: Kathy Ruiz
Senior Indexer: Cheryl Lenser
Senior Compositor: Gloria Schurick
Manufacturing Buyer: Dan Uhrig

© 2010 by Pearson Education, Inc.
Publishing as FT Press
Upper Saddle River, New Jersey 07458

This book is sold with the understanding that neither the author nor the publisher is engaged in rendering legal, accounting, or other professional services or advice by publishing this book. Each individual situation is unique. Thus, if legal or financial advice or other expert assistance is required in a specific situation, the services of a competent professional should be sought to ensure that the situation has been evaluated carefully and appropriately. The author and the publisher disclaim any liability, loss, or risk resulting directly or indirectly, from the use or application of any of the contents of this book.

FT Press offers excellent discounts on this book when ordered in quantity for bulk purchases or special sales. For more information, please contact U.S. Corporate and Government Sales, 1-800-382-3419, corpsales@pearsontechgroup.com. For sales outside the U.S., please contact International Sales at international@pearson.com.

Company and product names mentioned herein are the trademarks or registered trademarks of their respective owners.

Printed in the United States of America

Second Printing May 2010

ISBN-10: 0-13-702903-9
ISBN-13: 978-0-13-702903-7

Pearson Education LTD.
Pearson Education Australia PTY, Limited
Pearson Education Singapore, Pte. Ltd.
Pearson Education North Asia, Ltd.
Pearson Education Canada, Ltd.
Pearson Educatión de Mexico, S.A. de C.V.
Pearson Education—Japan
Pearson Education Malaysia, Pte. Ltd.

Library of Congress Cataloging-in-Publication Data

Augen, Jeffrey.

Day trading options : profiting from price distortions in very brief time frames / Jeff Augen.

p. cm.

ISBN-13: 978-0-13-702903-7 (hardback : alk. paper)

ISBN-10: 0-13-702903-9

1. Options (Finance)—United States. 2. Options (Finance) 3. Day trading (Securities) 4. Stock price forecasting. 5. Investment analysis. I. Title.

HG6024.A3A9217 2010

332.64—dc22

2009025835

On April 12, 1938, six thousand people crowded into Grand Central Station to watch Richard Whitney, former President of the New York Stock Exchange, being escorted off to Sing Sing prison by armed guards...

On June 29, 2009, applause rang out in a Manhattan courtroom as former NASDAQ Chairman, Bernard Madoff, was sentenced to 150 years in prison for engineering the largest Ponzi scheme in history...

This book is dedicated to the thousands of people who, over the years, have lost all their money to investment frauds. Serious investing is both complex and time consuming. There are no shortcuts—including letting others invest for you.

Contents

Acknowledgments

I'd like to thank the team that helped pull the book together. First and foremost is Jim Boyd who provided the opportunity and was willing to publish a new topic with an unusual focus.

Writing is easy. Making charts and tables is also easy. Creating a publication-quality book, however, is a different matter. Once again it has been my pleasure to work with Betsy Harris who was responsible for creating a final edited production document. In that regard I would also like to thank Cheri Clark who read every word and found many subtle and important mistakes.

Finally, I would like to acknowledge the excellent work of the Pearson marketing team and especially Julie Phifer and Laura Czaja who always seem willing to put real thought behind new book concepts.

Writing this book has been a real privilege because it allowed me to focus on controversial topics during a very unique time in financial history. Working with a team of focused professionals made the project possible.

About the Author

Jeff **Augen**, currently a private investor and writer, has spent more than a decade building a unique intellectual property portfolio of databases, algorithms, and associated software for technical analysis of derivatives prices. His work, which includes more than a million lines of computer code, is particularly focused on the identification of subtle anomalies and price distortions.

Augen has a 25-year history in information technology. As a cofounding executive of IBM's Life Sciences Computing business, he defined a growth strategy that resulted in $1.2 billion of new revenue and managed a large portfolio of venture capital investments. From 2002 to 2005, Augen was President and CEO of TurboWorx Inc., a technical computing software company founded by the chairman of the Department of Computer Science at Yale University. His books include *Trading Options at Expiration*, *The Option Trader's Workbook*, and *The Volatility Edge in Options Trading*. He currently teaches option trading classes at the New York Institute of Finance.

Preface

It is only fitting and proper that I write these words with a 1929 Conklin fountain pen—a gift from my wife. Most writers prefer a computer. I suppose that makes sense since it's where the words ultimately end up as a string of ones and zeros, but for me it's the Conklin. This pen has seen it all: the crash of '29, the great depression, World War II, Korea and Vietnam, the first Gulf War, another crash in 1987, Long Term Capital, 9/11 and the recession and war that followed, NASDAQ boom, NASDAQ bust, and most recently, the 2008–2009 banking crisis. I have a high level of respect for this old pen, and I'm always amazed at how smoothly it glides across the page as it undoubtedly did 80 years ago. Maybe there's a message in that effortless glide. Maybe some things never change.

Everyone knows that the market crashed in 1929. Back in those days, the private investor didn't have much of a chance. Big time stock manipulators drove prices into the stratosphere by selling to each other. When the price climbed high enough that the average investor finally jumped in, they dumped their stock, collected the profit, and watched the collapse. As always, the little guy took the hit because he was playing a game that he didn't understand.

Eighty years later, the game remains remarkably unchanged. The recent crash serves as a terrific illustration. Investment banks built high-risk portfolios of mortgage-backed derivatives, money poured in, bonuses flowed like water, and when it all collapsed the general public picked up the tab. Smart investors who saw the collapse coming and shorted the market lost money as the bubble inflated. Those who stayed in the market watched their money evaporate when the bubble burst. But many private investors—including the author of this book—did just fine. For the most part, they tended to be students of both the economy and the financial markets—active traders armed with a trading platform, charting software, and access to live news feeds.

These investors often believe that they can level the playing field by working hard and staying one step ahead of the market with a combination of the latest software and news sources. They often follow a combination of fundamental and technical indicators that include analyst statements, earnings reports, company news, insider transactions, short interest, and a few different types of price charts. Unfortunately, even the smartest and most diligent traders are further back in the pack than they might think. That is because the pack includes corporate insiders with much better information and institutional investors/analysts with direct access to the companies they invest in. Consider, for example, IBM—a heavily traded blue chip stock followed closely by many analysts and a large investment community. Between January 2008 and the end of May 2009 when these words were written, the average transaction price for IBM stock was $103.21. However, IBM insiders whose trades are publicly disclosed realized an average price of $122.65 in the open market—a 19% improvement.[1]

The difference is surprising because insiders are restricted with regard to when they can sell stock; in this sense they are disadvantaged and might be expected to realize a lower average selling price. Lifting all restrictions, therefore, might cause the gap to widen even further.

In either case the point is clear. A private investor with some charting software and a few analyst reports is no match for corporate insiders who know considerably more about their own company than the general public. The same private investor must also lose to large institutional analysts who have access to the companies they write about. Analysts routinely visit these companies and meet with key executives before writing their reports. Furthermore, their reports are proprietary and are often made available to a restricted group of subscribers or large clients of a particular brokerage. The playing field cannot be level when all investors do not have access to the same information.

Many investors who realize that they are operating at an information disadvantage avoid strategies that depend on fundamental business analysis and, instead, focus on purely technical approaches. Today's trading platforms accommodate this thinking with very sophisticated analytical tools. Dozens of technical indicators are available in addition to scripting languages that allow investors to create and test their own. Most platforms also allow automatic order entry based on a predefined set of rules. Serious traders can chart information in a variety of time frames and simultaneously analyze this information with different indicators. When a signal appears, their software can instantly place a trade without asking for confirmation. It would seem that such systems might have the potential to level the playing field for the private investor.

Unfortunately, the capability gap between institutional and private investors is even larger on the technical side than it is on the fundamental side; that difference is growing rapidly. During the past few years, computerized algorithmic trading systems have become the dominant force in most financial markets, and their sophistication exceeds anything available to the general public. Technical traders must now compete with supercomputers that process millions of data items each second and make investment decisions at the individual "tick" level. Such systems instantly identify and exploit emerging trends with the effect of extinguishing them almost as fast as they appear. Unfortunately for the private investor, this new dynamic has completely invalidated many approaches to technical analysis that worked well just a couple of years ago.

These changes are a logical evolution of the random walk hypothesis described by Burton Malkiel in his 1973 book entitled *A Random Walk Down Wall Street*. Simply stated, the random walk hypothesis asserts that the evolution of market prices cannot be predicted— that is, the recent price history of a stock does not contain information that can be used to predict its future. The random walk concept is built on an important set of assertions known as the efficient market hypothesis (EMH). EMH predicts that such inefficiencies cannot persist. It was first proposed by Eugene Fama in his Ph.D. thesis at the University of Chicago Graduate School of Business in the early 1960s. Since that time, there have been many debates between proponents of the theory and investors who believe that they can identify chart patterns with predictive power. However, for a chart pattern to have predictive power, it must also be persistent in the sense that the market cannot learn the pattern and eliminate it. Today's institutional trading systems settle any remaining argument by removing market inefficiencies at the millisecond level. The random walk model described by Burton Malkiel in his book assumes that stock price changes are tantamount to coin tosses. Our discussion will build on that concept by "over fitting" a technical indicator to a randomly generated stock chart and generating a set of rules that produce a surprisingly large return. The discussion is meant to illustrate the ease with which investors can be fooled by randomness.

Despite the disadvantages mentioned above, private option traders can profit in today's environment by entering and exiting the market at very specific times with trades that are structured to capitalize on well-characterized pricing anomalies and distortions. These opportunities exist, in part, because contemporary option pricing models assume continuous trading even though markets are closed over the weekend and from 4:00 PM to 9:30 AM each evening.

An efficient market can be expected to respond to these dynamics with price changes that comprehend the down time. Today's option market does just that by varying the implied volatility priced into option contracts to compensate for the distortions. These variations represent profit opportunity to an option trader and, as we shall see, the opportunity can become very large under certain circumstances. In this regard, we will review new approaches that separately measure overnight, intraday, and traditional volatility. These differences make it possible to capitalize on short-term anomalies where volatility is misrepresented in an option price. Finally, news events often introduce brief distortions that take many minutes for the market to digest. During these brief time frames the market becomes inefficient and new opportunities arise for the short-term trader. We will capitalize on these opportunities with a new technical indicator that can be used to quantify rising or falling volatility.

Investors who believe they have a trading system that consistently beats the market in all circumstances should read no further. This book was not written for them. It was written for investors who are seeking a different approach and are willing to work very hard to perfect new trading strategies. My goal was to find a way to narrow the performance gap that has plagued private investors since financial markets first opened.

Endnotes

1. Volume adjusted prices (VAP) were used to obtain maximum accuracy. Each transaction price was multiplied by the number of shares traded; results were summed and ultimately divided by the volume over the entire time frame. For the public market, each day's volume adjusted price was calculated using the average of the high+low and the day's volume. Insider trades are those reported on SEC form 4 and made available through Edgar Online. These transactions are readily available through many web-based sources including Yahoo! Finance.

Chapter 1

Basic Concepts

The Case for Short-Term Trading

This book is a product of one of the most challenging times in world financial history. Stated bluntly, the world's financial markets have become a gambling casino where equity, bond, commodity, and currency prices have virtually no predictable direction. Stock prices have become particularly unstable in the sense that they have virtually no relationship to the underlying performance of the company they represent. In the very week these words were written, the Dow fell 330 points on Tuesday, rallied 280 points on Wednesday, and fell another 250 points just after the open on Thursday morning. Worse still, the collapse on Tuesday was caused by a sell-off in financial stocks—the very stocks that fueled the rally the following day.

At the time of this writing, trillions of dollars had been lost by both bulls and bears. The markets were often described by both the financial press and national politicians as being in a "meltdown" with no end in sight. Investors who have never experienced a crashing market often believe that it is easy to generate profits in this environment with short positions. The result has been a new generation of exchange traded funds (ETFs) designed to rise when specific classes of investments fall. There are ETFs that short gold, oil, bonds, indexes, and equities in various sectors. Many are labeled "ultra-short" because they are structured to rise at twice the rate of decline of the underlying instruments. These investments are available to anyone with a brokerage account or an IRA and, unlike with traditional short positions, no margin is required. An investor can readily use these vehicles to short homebuilders, retail stores, banks, or just about any group of stocks, indexes, or financial instruments desired.

Many investors take a more precise approach by simply selling short financial instruments that they expect to decline in value. Markets move in both directions, and experienced investors recognize that money can be made on both sides. In bull markets they own stocks, and in bear markets they are often short the same stocks. Many investors prefer bear markets because the declines are often much steeper than the increases associated with a traditional bull market. Stated differently, markets can crash down but they rarely crash up.

These dynamics could easily lead to the mistaken conclusion that it is relatively easy to profit from a bear market by simply shorting distressed companies, sectors, or broad indexes that were previously overbought. Unfortunately, nothing is ever that simple. The 2008–2009 collapse included single-day bear market rallies as large as 11%—large enough to destroy virtually any short position. Many investors were fooled into believing that these rallies represented a market bottom and the beginning of a long-term recovery. They often took losses on their short positions by closing them and going long just in time for the next leg down of the market.

The answer lies in reducing market exposure by trading in very brief time frames. This approach flies in the face of conventional "buy and hold" wisdom. However, that approach has failed miserably because, as a group, investors have lost all their profits of the past decade. On January 22, 2009, the S&P 500 traded at its May 15, 1997, level. Subtracting an additional 30% for inflation and dollar devaluation paints an even darker, but more realistic, picture. Unfortunately, far too many investors have taken the wrong approach by remaining in the market with a portfolio of investments whether they were winning or losing. This approach has its own familiar vocabulary built around terms like "value investing," "diversification," and the all-too-familiar "buy and hold." As a group, long-term stock investors have suffered the greatest destruction of wealth in the history of the world.

Commodity traders face similar problems. In the brief time frame of just one year, both bulls and bears lost significant amounts of money as the price gained 50% from January to July 2008 before rapidly falling 72% to close the year below $40. Figure 1.1 traces the price from early January 2007 to early January 2009.

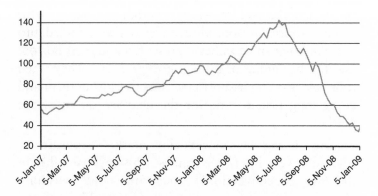

FIGURE 1.1   *Weekly Brent Blend spot price (USD) 2007/01/05 to 2009/01/05. Price is displayed on the y-axis, date on the x-axis. Source: U.S. Department of Energy, Energy Information Agency— http://www.eia.doe.gov.*

As always, timing is everything. But the more important lesson is that blindly hanging on with a bullish or bearish view is a flawed strategy. Every investment has a window of opportunity; unless that window can be identified, leaving the money invested is somewhat like gambling. That said, the window can be relatively long—sometimes spanning months or years.

Option trading in turbulent times can also be difficult. Implied volatilities rise sharply, making simple long put or call positions unreasonably expensive, and the risks associated with naked short positions are simply too large for any conservative investor. Structured positions, such as calendar spreads, ratios, and vertical spreads, are difficult to trade because stocks frequently cross several strike prices in a single month—sometimes in both directions.

Investors can avoid all these pitfalls by entering the market at very specific times and structuring trades that capitalize on well-characterized pricing anomalies and distortions. Option traders can use these distortions to structure positions that are both statistically advantaged and direction neutral. The most popular example being long straddles that have the potential to generate profit from a large price change in either direction. Investors who structure day trades that take advantage of these changes can generate more profit in one day than most experienced investors realize in an entire month—sometimes an entire year.

Unlike other trading strategies that are linked—sometimes in subtle ways—to a specific set of market conditions, options day trading focuses only on the underlying mathematics. It does not rely on any financial predictions, company results, or market direction. In this context a day trader manages ticker symbols and strike prices because the name or business of the underlying stock is mostly irrelevant. But nothing worth doing is ever easy. Trading subtle price distortions in the options market is a complex affair that requires an unusual blend of pricing knowledge and trading skill. Day trading is a mathematical game distinctly different from stock picking. Its potential gains, however, are enormous—far greater than those of any "long-term" strategy.

That said, short-term trading strategies can also be simple. It is often possible to simply trade the news. For example, on March 30, 2009, the president of the United States, Barack Obama, bluntly rejected turnaround plans submitted by General Motors Corp. and

Chrysler LLC, and demanded fresh concessions for long-term federal aid. He also raised the possibility of bankruptcy for either or both of the ailing auto giants. While the content of the speech could not have been known in advance, the fact that the speech was scheduled was announced before the market close on Friday, March 27. In addition, statements made over the weekend by Treasury Secretary Timothy Geithner further underscored investor fear that the financial industry's troubles were far from over. He stated that several banks would likely need considerably more money to survive. Once again the timing of the statement, but not the content, was widely known before the market close on Friday.

A short-term trader who anticipated that these events would have a large impact on the market could have purchased an at-the-money straddle on the Dow using the Diamonds Trust exchange traded fund (ticker: DIA).[1] At the close on Friday, DIA traded for $77.81 and the $78 straddle cost $5.12 ($2.49 call/$2.63 put). Following the negative news on Monday, the Dow fell more than 4% and DIA traded as low as $74.37. At the low, the $78 straddle traded for $5.77 ($1.08 call/$4.69 put)—a 12.7% gain. Had our trader missed the low and held on until the close, he would still have realized a profit by selling the straddle for $5.55.

As we have just seen, options provide a distinct advantage because they allow the construction of direction-neutral positions. This dynamic distinctly changes the character of short-term trading. Option traders can decide that a position is underpriced because it does not adequately represent the risk of an upcoming news event. This view then forms the basis of a structured position that can profit from a large swing in either direction. In our March 30 example, if the news had not generated a large market swing, we would have risked only a very small amount of weekend time decay in the option premium. This effect is further diminished for trades placed near the closing bell because option prices tend to shrink near the close on Friday as the market discounts weekend time decay into the price—that is, implied volatility tends to decrease on Friday afternoon. In broad terms, the trade was relatively riskless and very brief.

Option day traders can also profit from implied volatility swings—a distinct advantage unique to the options world. An excellent example arose just as these words were being written. The April 2009 expiration week began on Easter Sunday and the market was closed on the preceding Friday—Good Friday. The long weekend was very significant because it represented three of the remaining seven days in the expiration cycle. Option buyers were predictably hesitant to over-pay for contracts that were about to lose a significant amount of value while the market was closed. The result was persistently falling implied volatility from the open to the close on Thursday, April 9. For example, implied volatility for at-the-money options on Research in Motion (ticker: RIMM) declined steadily from 65% at the open to 50% at the close. This decline was entirely predictable; it exactly offset the weekend time decay so that a return to 65% implied volatility on Monday just restored option prices to their closing values on Thursday. As a result, investors who purchased

RIMM call options at the close on Thursday were not penalized for the three days that the market remained closed.

This efficiency of the market represented a tremendous trading opportunity because it condensed three days of time decay near the end of an expiration cycle into a single trading day. A simple structured position consisting of 10 long $60 calls and 20 short $65 calls returned more than 80%—the trade cost $0.89 at the open and sold for $1.61 at the close with the stock price nearly unchanged (the stock opened at $63.99 and closed at $64.18—a move of just $0.19). Day trading the stock would have been very difficult because it would have required precise timing to capitalize on intraday price changes. Day trading the option was simple; it required nothing more than opening a position in the morning and closing it in the afternoon. Moreover, the trade generated a steadily growing profit throughout the day as implied volatility collapse followed a straight path with a steep slope of 2.3% per hour. An aggressive investor who understood the phenomenon could have generated more profit in a single day than most skilled traders realize in an entire year with no overnight risk and very limited market exposure. We will return to a more detailed discussion of this phenomenon in Chapter 5, "Special Events."

Recent Changes in the Options Market Support Day Trading

Until recently, day trading options was difficult because bid-ask spreads were large, and contract liquidity was often limited. Those dynamics have changed dramatically. The markets have deployed penny pricing programs that all but eliminate bid-ask spreads, and options volume has soared in recent years. Heavily traded stocks typically have enough options volume to support even the wealthiest private investors creating multimillion-dollar positions. Additionally, improvements in trading platforms have completely leveled the playing field between large institutions and private day traders. An individual sitting at his or her desk at home can experience the same rapid execution and instant price updates as the largest institutional investor on the floor of the exchange. Contemporary trading platforms also provide access to sophisticated charting tools as well as the level II trading queue. This level of access allows a private investor to view the activities of individual market makers trading on different exchanges, and to take advantage of subtle and fleeting changes in bid-ask spreads. For example, near the end of a brief but significant rally, buyers often become less aggressive and lower their bid prices, causing the bid-ask spread to widen. This change is often a better indicator that a rally is ending than any identifiable chart pattern. Savvy day traders who watch the level II queue often capitalize on this opportunity to sell options that quickly lose value if the stock reverses direction and corrects slightly downward.

Private investors trading relatively small numbers of contracts also have an advantage because their trades are usually executed using the "best" bid and ask prices. They typically outperform institutional investors who place very large trades that cannot be filled from the top of the queue. The difference affects both pricing and execution. A private investor sitting in front of a computer can open and close small trades consisting of just a few contracts with the simple click of a mouse. His institutional counterpart trading thousands or tens of thousands of contracts does not have that luxury.

The distance between strike prices is also important to option traders. Traditionally the spacing has been set at $2.50 for stocks under $25; $5.00 when the strike price is between $25 and $200; and $10.00 for strikes over $200. Each of the exchanges is currently experimenting with $1.00 spacing for stocks up to $50 and $2.50 spacing for stocks up to $75. Increasing the number of strikes and reducing the spacing makes it easier for option traders to precisely calibrate their position structures. These changes are particularly important to day traders as they attempt to structure positions that profit from relatively small underlying price changes. Long straddles are an excellent example because they should be initiated only with the stock trading close to a strike price where put and call deltas are equal. Day traders seeking to launch long straddles must often wait for the right conditions to avoid placing trades with a directional character. Closer strike price spacing helps solve this problem by increasing the probability of a stock trading at a relatively delta-neutral price.

Unstable Markets Provide Unique Advantages to Option Traders

Excessive market turmoil has also changed the dynamics of option pricing in three specific ways:

1. Higher implied volatility across all option contracts

2. Steepened implied volatility skew from low to high strike prices

3. Large implied volatility swings (implied volatility has become more volatile)

The turmoil is apparent in Figure 1.2, which depicts the CBOE Volatility Index (VIX) from July 2008 to February 2009. The value of the index more than doubled from just over 20 in September 2008 to near 50 at the right side of the chart. The index spiked as high as 80, completely destabilizing option prices, during the rapid market collapse that took place between early October and late November 2008.

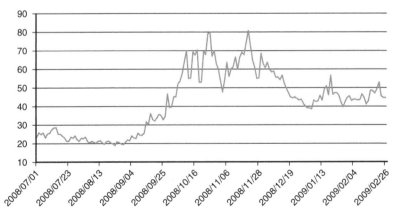

FIGURE 1.2   *The VIX from July 2008 to February 2009.*

These changes represent new opportunities for option traders who structure complex trades encompassing a variety of strike prices and expirations.

Option prices were stable and low during the pre-crash phase visible at the left side of the chart. This era was characterized by very limited strike price choices because far strikes had little to no value for options expiring in the current month. The differences are apparent in the implied volatilities priced into various near-expiration options for Goldman Sachs before and after the market collapse. Table 1.1 lists implied volatilities for options below and above the stock price on 7/28/2008, 19 days before the August 2008 expiration. Table 1.2 provides a similar list for the March 2009 expiration (implied volatilities on 3/2/2009, 19 days before expiration).

TABLE 1.1   *Pre-Crash Implied Volatilities for Goldman Sachs Options Prior to the August 2008 Expiration (Stock price = $172.90 with 19 days remaining before expiration.)*

Put Strike	Implied Volatility (%)	Call Strike	Implied Volatility (%)
140	63	170	48
145	59	175	45
150	57	180	42
155	54	185	40
160	51	190	38
165	47	195	38
170	45		

TABLE 1.2 *Post-Crash Implied Volatilities for Goldman Sachs Options Prior to the March 2009 Expiration (Stock price = $86.85 with 19 days remaining before expiration.)*

Put Strike	Implied Volatility (%)	Call Strike	Implied Volatility (%)
50	145	85	91
55	136	90	87
60	126	95	82
65	119	100	78
70	112	105	75
75	106	110	73
80	100		
85	95		
90	92		

The differences are striking. Before the large market decline, at-the-money implied volatilities were stable in the 45% range. In the post-crash era, however, implied volatility for at-the-money options was as high as 95%. In percentage terms, the skew between at-the-money and out-of-the-money options was surprisingly flat between the two sets. In the pre-crash era, put volatility grew by 40% from 45% to 63% across six strikes. After the crash, implied volatility grew 43% across six strikes from 95% to 136%. However, in absolute value terms, implied volatility increased much more dramatically after the crash. This distortion creates a much steeper price curve.

The steepness of the second curve is apparent in Table 1.3, which displays prices for the put options listed in Table 1.2 and calculated values for the same options using half the actual implied volatility.

TABLE 1.3   *Left Side: Post-Crash Implied Volatilities and Prices for Goldman Sachs Put Options Prior to the March 2009 Expiration; Right Side: Calculated Values for the Same Options with Implied Volatility Reduced by Half (Stock price = 86.85 with 19 days remaining before expiration, risk-free interest rate = 1.5%.)*

Put Strike	Implied Volatility #1 (%)	Price #1 ($)	Implied Volatility #2 (%)	Price #2 ($)
50	145	0.44	73	0.00
55	136	0.68	68	0.01
60	126	0.99	63	0.02
65	119	1.51	60	0.06
70	112	2.24	56	0.19
75	106	3.28	53	0.54
80	100	4.67	50	1.32
85	95	6.56	48	2.86
90	92	9.09	46	5.47

The differences become striking when values for out-of-the-money options are compared. With implied volatilities reduced by half, it becomes impractical to structure trades that involve selling $50, $55, $60, $65, or $70 strike prices. These estimates are reasonable because at-the-money options in the pre-crash market traded for slightly less than half their post-crash values ($170 put = 45% implied before the drawdown; $85 put = 95% implied volatility after the drawdown). Differences in the shapes of the two curves are revealed in Figure 1.3.

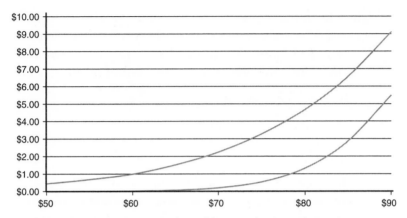

FIGURE 1.3   *Price curves for Goldman Sachs put options prior to the March 2009 expiration. The steeper curve represents actual prices; the flatter curve traces values for the same options with implied volatility reduced by half at each strike. Strike prices are displayed on the x-axis, put option prices on the y-axis.*

The environment of the steeper curve is highly beneficial to option traders because it allows complex positions to be structured across many strikes. It also increases liquidity. Referring to Table 1.3, only four put strikes are likely to be tradable in the reduced volatility example on the right side of the table, while the actual situation facilitated trading across all nine strikes listed on the left side ($50 to $90). This result is surprising because only 19 days remained before expiration. A conservative investor could have structured a ratio trade consisting of 10 long $55 puts and 20 short $50 puts with absolutely no risk unless the stock fell from $86.85 to below $45.00 in the remaining two weeks. The trade would have yielded a maximum return of $4.80 with the stock expiring at the short strike ($50). In most cases an investor would expect such a trade to expire with both sides out-of-the-money. These dynamics hint at a more aggressive solution that involves 30 short $50 puts and 10 long $55 puts. Assuming that both sides expire worthless, the trade would generate $640 of profit:

30 short $50 puts × $0.44 = $1,320

10 long $55 puts × $0.68 = $680

Net short   = $640

Although this return might seem small, it dramatically exceeds any interest-generating investment in the post-crash environment where the Fed Funds target rate was set at 0.00% to 0.25%. More precisely, the return on this trade would be equal to the profit ($640) divided by the total cost for the long side ($680 for 10 contracts) plus the margin requirement for the 20 naked short puts ($18,010):[2]

$640 / ($680 + $18,010) = .034

Considering that the trade was open for only 19 days, the return in percentage terms (3.4%) is surprisingly large. Moreover, had the stock fallen to a point between the long and short strikes, the trade would have generated a much larger return. Optimally, with the stock trading at $50 on expiration day, the position would be worth $5.00 ($5,000 for 10 long $55 puts that are $5 in-the-money), and the profit would be $5,640 calculated as the final value of the trade plus $640 obtained from the original net short position. Total profit would rise to 30%, albeit an unlikely scenario.

We can extend these calculations using 30-day prices to project a monthly return. A variety of positions can be structured using the three lowest strikes on our list:

$50 put = $1.17 @ 145% implied volatility

$55 put = $1.60 @ 136% implied volatility

$60 put = $2.07 @ 126% implied volatility

We could, for example, structure a 2:1 ratio composed of 20 short $50 puts and 10 long $55 puts. This position would be fully protected down to an underlying price of $45. The more aggressive trade outlined previously could be duplicated using 30 short $50 puts and 10 long $55 puts. Although not as well protected in a deep crash of the stock, this trade delivers a significantly larger return. The answer is most likely a hybrid of the two choices. We can construct such a trade using a 3:1 ratio that is short $50 puts and long $60 puts. The position, therefore, would be net short $1.44 as shown here:

30 short $50 puts at $1.17	=	$3,510
10 long $60 puts at $2.07	=	$2,070
Net short	=	$1,440

If the stock closes expiration above both strikes, the trade will generate a minimum return of 7.2% during the 30 days remaining before expiration:

$1,440 / ($2,070 + $18,010) = .072

Monthly compounding of this conservative trade would, therefore, generate an annual return of 144%. As before, each monthly version of the trade would be far more profitable if the stock fell far enough to close expiration between the long and short strikes. At the short strike, the position would generate an $11,440 profit calculated as $10,000 for the long $60 put plus the original short sale of $1,440—a total monthly return of 57%. A more likely scenario, however, would be for the stock to settle in the $10 space between the two strikes. If, for example, the stock closed expiration at $55, the long $60 put would be worth $5.00 and the profit would be $6,440 calculated as $5,000 plus the value of the original net short position ($1,440):

$6,440 / ($2,070 + $18,010) = .321

This return is reasonable because the stock is very likely to land in this large region between the strikes and the required movement is not particularly large. Calculated in standard deviations using at-the-money implied volatility of 95%, a 1-month 1 standard deviation price change would be $23.82:

$86.85 × 0.95 / SQRT(12) = $23.82

The distance to $55, the midpoint between the strikes, is $31.85 or 1.3 standard deviations. Option pricing theory, built on the normal distribution, sets the probability of this downward price change at 9.7%. The value can be obtained using an Excel spreadsheet and the NORMSDIST function.[3] Unfortunately, taken out of context, this particular value is not helpful because it represents the probability of a precise change from the starting price to exactly $55. A more reasonable approach would be to calculate the probability of the stock closing expiration in various trading ranges with distinct profit characteristics. The following list includes the four most significant ranges for this trade, which are further quantified in Table 1.4:

1. Above both strikes ($60) where the initial $1.44 of excess premium is retained as profit

2. Between the upper ($60) and lower ($50) strikes—
   the so-called "profit zone" where the trade returns
   more than the initial net short amount of $1.44

3. Between the lower strike ($50) and the break-even
   point ($45.70) where profit shrinks below the initial
   net short amount of $1.44

4. Beyond the break-even point ($45.70) where the
   trade loses money

A determination of the exact break-even point
referenced in list items 3 and 4 must include the excess
$1.44 of premium realized from the initial position
structure—that is, the final break-even point must be
adjusted to remove this initial gain.[4]

TABLE 1.4 *Risk Assessment for the 3:1 Ratio Trade Described
Previously (30 short $50 puts and 10 long $60 puts for Goldman
Sachs with 30 days remaining before the March 2009 expiration.
Calculations are based on the normal distribution.)*

Description	Result	Probability
Stock closes expiration above $60 strike price	Trade profit = $1,440 (7.2%)	87.0%
Stock closes expiration in the profit zone between the long ($60) and short ($50) strikes	Trade profit between $1,440 (7.2%) and $11,440 (57%)	6.9%
Stock closes expiration between the short strike ($50) and the break-even point ($45.70)	Trade profit shrinks to a value between $0.00 and $1,440	1.9%
Stock closes expiration below the break-even point ($45.70)	Trade loses money at the rate of $2,000 for each additional dollar of underlying price decline	4.2%

Based on the characteristics outlined in Table 1.4, the trade has an excellent risk:return profile. Most of the advantage accrues from the steep implied volatility smile that allows us to sell 145% volatility while purchasing only 126%. The skew—or "smile," as it is often called—is a response to a crashing market in which large amounts of money can be lost by investors who sell out-of-the-money puts. The smile first became steep after the 1987 crash that took the market down 25% in a single day. Since then, implied volatility profiles for equity and index options have taken on a distinctly negative skew—that is, volatility tends to rise as the strike price decreases. This effect causes out-of-the-money puts to be relatively more expensive than traditional option pricing theory predicts. Additionally, since put-call parity dictates that the relationship between strike price and implied volatility be the same for both types of contracts, in-the-money calls should also be more expensive. Far out-of-the-money call prices normally flatten out with implied volatility stabilizing several strike prices above the trading price of the stock. This flattening is what gives rise to a curve with a shape that can be referred to as a smile.

The smile also allows us to create a deep out-of-the-money short position with options that would be illiquid and nearly worthless if priced using the much lower at-the-money implied volatility of 95%. These dynamics make it difficult to structure a similar trade with call options because the volatility skew disproportionately increases the price of the long strike over the short strike. Bear market volatility skews generally favor trades that are structured with short components at lower strikes.

Summarizing the data outlined in Table 1.4, we can conclude that the trade will most likely deliver a significant profit (94% probability of returning more than 7.2% on invested capital). Only 4.2% of trades are likely to lose money. Furthermore, because the trade is structured with deep out-of-the-money options that have significant amounts of remaining time premium, it is very likely that outsized downward spikes can be handled through adjustments to the original position. At this level of analysis, the trade appears to be mathematically sound.

These calculations would be valid in most markets. However, the instability that gave rise to a steep volatility skew and allowed us to structure a profitable low-risk trade is also disruptive from an option pricing perspective. The sharp increase in out-of-the-money put prices is likely to be too small to accommodate a sharp downward spike. The problem is illustrated in Table 1.5, which displays the high, low, and number of strike prices crossed during 15 expirations of Goldman Sachs stock options.

TABLE 1.5   *High, Low, and Number of Strikes Crossed for Goldman Sachs Stock During 15 Expirations (January 2008–March 2009) (Periods of rapid decline and high implied volatility are highlighted in gray.)*

Expiration	Start Date	End Date	High	Low	Strikes
Jan-08	2007/12/23	2008/01/19	217.80	183.70	5
Feb-08	2008/01/20	2008/02/16	208.78	173.37	6
Mar-08	2008/02/17	2008/03/22	181.37	140.27	8
Apr-08	2008/03/23	2008/04/19	184.52	161.68	4
May-08	2008/04/20	2008/05/17	203.39	178.00	5
Jun-08	2008/05/18	2008/06/21	189.32	161.21	5
Jul-08	2008/06/22	2008/07/19	187.01	152.25	7
Aug-08	2008/07/20	2008/08/16	190.04	162.34	6
Sep-08	2008/08/17	2008/09/20	172.45	85.88	17
Oct-08	2008/09/21	2008/10/18	142.00	74.00	14
Nov-08	2008/10/19	2008/11/22	123.80	47.41	15
Dec-08	2008/11/23	2008/12/20	81.29	55.27	5
Jan-09	2008/12/21	2009/01/17	92.20	69.00	5
Feb-09	2009/01/18	2009/02/21	98.66	59.13	8
Mar-09	2009/02/22	2009/03/21	106.79	72.78	7

Three expirations involved extraordinary price changes. The most extreme (September 2008) spanned 17 strikes. These three expirations, highlighted in gray, each involved price changes approximately twice as large as anticipated in our trading example. Using the same 19-day time frame, implied volatility for the lowest strike price in the example ($50) would need to rise above 500% to comprehend the September change. This value is estimated by taking the percentage of time in the options cycle represented by 19 days (approximately 63%) and multiplying by the magnitude of the full month swing ($86.57 for September). The result implies a price change of $55. Assuming the same starting point of $86.85, a $55 decline would place the $50 puts more than $18 in-the-money with the stock trading at $31.85. Using a Black-Scholes option pricing calculator, we can determine that implied volatility would be 589% for a $50 put priced at $18 with 19 days remaining before expiration (risk-free interest set at 1.5%). The sharp implied volatility skew present during the March 2009 expiration cycle would have been insufficient protection against the price swings of September, October, and November 2008. Moreover, investors who structured September trades based on the price change behavior displayed during August would have suffered severe losses because the September volatility skew was insufficient to cope with the price drop that was about to occur.

This discussion highlights the risks associated with structuring trades in an unstable market where virtually anything can happen. As it turned out, Goldman Sachs rallied to close the March expiration at $97.32 with every strike price listed in Table 1.3 far out-of-the-money. However, October and November involved steep declines that were not entirely comprehended by the options market despite the 17 strike price move of the September expiration.

During this highly turbulent time, financial markets became unstable as the United States government began pouring hundreds of billions of dollars into failed banking institutions. Each day was characterized by startling news—Merrill Lynch and Bear Stearns were purchased by traditional banks (Bank of America and JPMorgan, respectively) while Lehman Brothers went bankrupt, bringing an end to the era of independent investment banking on Wall Street. During the same time frame, the world discovered that insurance giant AIG was insolvent, and that the U.S. government would be forced to bail out the company in exchange for an equity stake. Short-term trading during this time of confusion was highly profitable.

Virtually every day presented excellent opportunities for day traders of financial stocks. In many cases the particular day for a trade could have been selected by watching the financial news. For example, Goldman Sachs—the stock highlighted previously—fell from $127.51 to $112.02 on October 7 after the announcement of a U.S. government–sponsored rescue plan caused the overnight collapse of all Asian markets, and Alcoa Aluminum announced a 52% drop in profits. The Dow fell 500 points with concentrated losses in the financial sector. Two days later, on October 9, Goldman fell from a high of $118.94 to $100.00 when a three-week-old short selling ban on all financial stocks was lifted by the SEC.

Overnight trades were also highly profitable. The close-to-open gap between September 16 and September 17 was an excellent example. On September 16, the government announced its first $85 billion bailout of AIG. That news coupled with the collapse of Lehman Brothers and Merrill Lynch triggered sharp declines across the globe in overnight trading. The next day, September 17, was marked by a 450-point decline in the Dow. Once again, Goldman Sachs was impacted. The stock closed September 16 trading at 133.01 and opened the next day at 120.94. Large as it might seem, this decline was much smaller than the intraday move that took the stock to a low of $97.78—an additional 23-point decline.

Structured trades designed to profit from sharp downward spikes do exceptionally well during times of such instability. Put backspreads are excellent examples. A perfect candidate at the close on September 16 would have been a position consisting of 20 long $120 puts and 10 short $130 puts. In the initial position, both long and short positions would have cost approximately the same. When the stock plunged to $97.78, the short side would have been $32.22 in-the-money, and the twice-as-large long side would have been $22.22 in-the-money. Setting aside time premium, the short side would have been worth $32.22 and the long side $44.44 for a total profit of $12.22, or $12,220 for every 10 contracts sold. The day trade, based on the previous evening's news, was highly profitable in an environment that would have been destructive to many long-term structured positions. In this case, a put backspread with a neutral initial cost was used to guard against a sharp rise in the stock price. Many other trades such as long straddles, long strangles, or covered puts (short stock combined with short puts) were also reasonable candidates. More aggressive investors would have simply purchased puts or shorted the stock. Another popular trade for bearish investors involves buying far out-of-the-money puts and paying for the trade by selling equally far out-of-the-money calls. The position generates neither profit nor loss as long as the stock remains between the strikes until expiration. However, in the event of a sharp downward spike like that of September 17, the trade can return profits in the hundreds of percent.

Technical Analysis, Technical Indicators, and Price Distortions

This book explores day trading strategies that are distinctly different from traditional approaches that depend on predicting the direction of movement of a stock or an index. Most traditional day trading systems rely on a combination of technical indicators to signal entry and exit points for trades. Unfortunately, today's markets have become very fast and efficient, making it difficult to gain an advantage that persists long enough to trade. These efficiency gains have been driven by hundreds of thousands of active traders who are now using sophisticated platforms for rule-based trading. During the past few years, these platforms have become key differentiators for brokers attracting an ever-growing population of sophisticated online investors. The latest generation typically includes a scripting language for the development of custom indicators in addition to dozens of standard chart types that can easily be modified. Most systems also include back testing and optimization tools. At any given moment, millions of private investors around the world are using such platforms to spot entry and exit points for specific types of trades.

In addition to the millions of private investors, large institutions and hedge funds constantly exploit very subtle market changes with algorithmic trading systems that can react almost instantly. In principle, an algorithmic trading system uses a sequence of steps to test and recognize patterns in real-time market data. When a trading opportunity is detected, the system places and manages the appropriate order. Many of these systems are designed to spot short-lived arbitrages that allow an investor to realize a profit from slight pricing differences between markets. Most of these arbitrages exist for only a few seconds before market efficiencies extinguish them. To create a reliable technical indicator that can be used to repeatedly generate a profit, you must discover a market inefficiency that is fundamentally the same as an arbitrage. Discovering such an inefficiency in today's markets using traditional charting techniques is difficult at best. Worse still, if you were to discover an indicator that reliably predicts the direction of a stock's next move, its use would quickly erase the inefficiency that originally allowed it to work.

Recent advances in the algorithmic trading space have been impressive. In the past, traders manually built, tested, and managed their trading strategies. They tracked various analytics by watching charts simultaneously displayed across several screens. When a signal was detected, they placed a trade and managed its execution manually. Today's systems allow institutional traders to simultaneously monitor a large number of different algorithmic systems using a graphical display that is somewhat like a dashboard. Rather than selecting individual trades, modern institutional traders spend much of their time working with quantitative analysts to fine-tune algorithmic systems.

At the time of this writing, IBM in collaboration with TD Securities was in the process of deploying an algorithmic trading system prototype it described as "the world's fastest automated options trading system."[5,6]

The new approach enables rapid, intelligent analysis of live streaming data from a large number of sources. It combines supercomputing horsepower with advanced data stream management software to cope with information volumes that often exceed two million messages per second. As with any automated trading system, the goal is to reduce the time between the receipt of market data and the final trading decision. By achieving lower latency and higher data rates, the new system can respond to market situations before they can be detected by other institutional investors.

Such systems have created unprecedented levels of market efficiency. The results are apparent in Table 1.6, which reveals information about the link between consecutive minutes across one year of trading for the S&P 500 using the exchange traded fund SPDR Trust (ticker: SPY).[7] The left side of the table contains information about "up" minutes; the right side contains the same information about "down" minutes. Threshold values for the first minute of each pair are contained in column #1 (First-Minute Change). In each case, the second minute is not required to meet the same threshold as the first—any move in the same direction is recorded as a "repeat."

TABLE 1.6   *Number of Minutes Repeating the Direction of a Previous Minute for One Year of the SPDR Trust (SPY) (The first column indicates the threshold used to filter the first minute. The data spans 102,272 minutes beginning on 2008/04/09 and ending on 2009/04/09.)*

First-Minute Change	Up Minutes	Repeat Up	Repeat Up Avg.	Down Minutes	Repeat Down	Repeat Down Avg.
0.1%	11,434	5,193	0.454	11,617	5,363	0.462
0.2%	3,542	1,608	0.454	3,512	1,654	0.471
0.3%	1,303	591	0.454	1,178	590	0.501
0.4%	531	238	0.448	462	228	0.494
0.5%	233	108	0.464	201	96	0.478
0.6%	114	50	0.439	92	43	0.467
0.7%	56	25	0.446	53	24	0.453

The results are striking. In every case, regardless of the threshold, the direction of movement for the second minute is unrelated to the first. Even in the most extreme case, where the price change threshold for the first minute is set at 0.7%, the chance that the next minute will contain a price change in the same direction is only 45% for both up and down directions. This example is especially noteworthy because only 56 up minutes and 53 down minutes met the criterion out of a population of 102,272 minutes. These rare examples represent unique moments when the market experienced a large directional move greater than 0.7% in just one minute. It is surprising, therefore, that the next minute's direction cannot be predicted. Moreover, additional data that will be discussed in the next chapter reveals that the lack of predictability persists long after a large price change; the direction of the market 10 minutes later is also random under these circumstances. The implication is that the market responds to news so quickly that the complete response tends to be contained in a single minute. This behavior seems to hold true for even the largest price changes.

As we shall see, these dynamics are consistent for individual stocks, indexes, and the broad market. They are also apparent in data sets that span a broad range of time frames ranging from one minute to several days. The implications of these simple facts are far-reaching, and they weigh heavily against many highly regarded forms of technical analysis. Consider, for example, the situation in which an unusually reliable technical indicator can predict with 100% certainty that a large price spike is about to occur. According to the data, the probability that the market will continue to move in the same direction is random. Simply stated, in an efficient market, a stock price has no memory. It reacts to breaking news, rumors, and the activities of millions of traders on a moment-to-moment basis. Each moment begins anew at the current price.

Fortunately, these assertions do not invalidate technical analysis or charting. However, they raise the bar considerably by questioning whether the recent price history of a stock encodes information that can be used to predict its future direction. The discussion must be expanded to include a variety of complex indicators across many different financial markets. Examples include, but are not limited to, fixed income, foreign exchange, precious metals, agricultural commodities, oil, stock and index futures, volatility options and futures, and dozens of indexes that track metrics for stock exchanges around the world. Institutional trading systems based on complex algorithms are a perfect example because they often exploit a set of indicators specific to a variety of financial instruments, markets, and time frames. These systems are built with enormous amounts of historical data, and they are constantly adjusted to fit changing market conditions. Moreover, they are often designed to exploit market inefficiencies that persist for just a few seconds, and to generate very small profits that accumulate over time. For private investors, competing against these systems is difficult with even the most powerful trading platforms.

Institutional trading systems are sometimes optimized to exploit a specific distortion between markets. Such was the case during most of 2006 and 2007 when the "yen carry trade" persisted as a major driving force in world financial markets. Investors routinely borrowed Japanese yen at ultralow interest rates and invested the money in gold and U.S. stocks. As a result, the Dow climbed from 10,500 to 14,000 and gold skyrocketed from $500 to $1,000. The forces were complex because they involved emergency-level interest rates in the U.S., rising demand for commodities in China and India, international trade issues including an exploding U.S. trade deficit that hovered near $800 billion, a growing bubble in the fixed income markets, a collapsing dollar, and a dramatic escalation in the price of virtually all assets—especially real estate. Institutional investors responded, on a minute-by-minute basis, to subtle changes in foreign exchange rates by moving billions of dollars in and out of markets to optimize their return on capital. The goal was always to generate as much profit as possible in the most promising markets using borrowed yen, and to pay back the loans at just the right time to avoid losing money to a strengthening yen or a falling dollar. The technical indicators necessary to understand this market were enormously complex and the time frame in which they needed to be monitored was very brief. Furthermore, algorithms needed to be constantly adapted to changing market conditions. Investors who did not understand the yen carry trade, or did not include appropriate information about currency and interest rate markets in their technical analysis, were disadvantaged in their trading. Those who did were competing directly with institutional investors capable of moving around large blocks of money very quickly.

A much more realistic approach is to take advantage of occasional pricing inefficiencies that arise in the options market. These distortions can be related to earnings announcements, expiration week, weekend time decay, intraday implied volatility swings, differences between overnight and intraday volatility, or news and rumors. We have already seen simple, but powerful, examples of these distortions in the form of the market's reaction to the March 30, 2009, presidential announcement about the automobile industry, and the April 2009 three-day Easter weekend that preceded expiration week. The later example caused an unavoidable price distortion that generated an 80% return in a single day.

Private investors can learn to capitalize on such distortions to generate very large returns with relatively little risk. They can also leverage the advances that have been achieved in trading platforms to capture as much profit as possible from efficient execution. Combined with narrow bid-ask spreads and high levels of liquidity, these advances have created unprecedented opportunities for private investors who want to exploit the technical advantages and financial leverage of options while trading in the time frame of a single day. Nothing in the investment world can rival the simplicity of opening and closing a trade in just a few hours, taking home nothing more than cash when the market closes, and starting again fresh the very next day.

Endnotes

1. The Diamonds Trust seeks to provide investment results that, before expenses, generally correspond to the price and yield performance of the Dow Jones Industrial Average (DJIA).

2. Margin requirements for deep out-of-the-money naked short options are calculated as 10% of the value of the underlying stock represented by the naked short options plus the actual value of the options sold. In this case the requirement would be (0.10 × 20 contracts × 100 shares per contract × $86.85 + $640 value of options sold = $18,010).

3. This value can be obtained using an Excel's NORMSDIST function. For a 1.3 standard deviation change NORMSDIST(1.3) = .9032. This value represents the percentage of price changes that fall behind a 1.3 standard deviation price change on one side (plus or minus) of the distribution curve. In this case, all price changes in the positive (up) direction plus any price change smaller than 1.3 standard deviations in the negative (down) direction are included in the 90.32%. Subtracting from 1.00,

therefore, yields the probability of a 1.3 standard deviation directional change. $1.00 - 0.9032 = 0.0968$ or 9.68%. Because this value represents the probability of a 1.3 standard deviation change in one direction, multiplying by 2 yields the chance that the price will move 1.3 standard deviations in either direction (19.36%).

4. The break-even point is calculated in this way: At expiration, with the stock below the strike price, the long side of the trade will be worth $60 - X - $1.40 where X is the trading price of the stock. The short side of the trade will be worth $3(50 - X)$. We can, therefore, write the relationship as $58.60 - X = $150 - 3X$. Solving for X gives a break-even price of $45.70. This value includes the $1.40 realized from the original sale of short $50 puts.

5. "IBM Unveils Prototype of Fast Financial Analysis System," *Automated Trader,* April 14, 2009.

6. "IBM Unveils Prototype of World's Fastest Financial Analysis System," IBM press release, April 9, 2009.

7. SPDR Trust is an exchange traded fund that holds all the S&P 500 Index stocks.

Chapter 2

New Directions in Automated Trading

Key Concepts

- High-performance computing systems capable of identifying and trading subtle market inefficiencies have come into widespread use in the financial community. These systems react to changing market conditions at the tick level.

- The combined activities of automated high-performance trading systems extinguish market inefficiencies almost immediately. Private investors using off-the-shelf software cannot react quickly enough to compete in this environment.

- Statistical analysis of minute-by-minute price changes supports these assertions. Studies reveal that large price changes do not result in persistent trends—even at the single-minute level. Stated differently, the recent price history of a stock does not contain enough information to predict the direction.

- Persistent trends exist at the tick level, where they can be exploited by institutional investors who repeatedly capture very small profits in very brief time frames.

- Technical traders sometimes "over fit" indicators and rules to a stock chart. This problem can be illustrated by selecting a set of rules that generate outstanding profits from a randomly generated chart.

- Insider trading is a significant market force. Option traders can often spot trends that reveal the behavior of insiders. This knowledge can be used to place profitable trades.

- Option traders can take advantage of volatility distortions and other pricing anomalies that cannot be extinguished by normal market forces.

High-Performance Computing and Market Efficiency

Today's markets are fundamentally different from those of just three or four years ago. Most of these changes have been driven by explosive growth in computing horsepower coupled with improved high-speed communications links and exotic software for managing multiple data streams. These advances have created an environment in which computer programs routinely exploit the most subtle price inefficiencies and trends to capture very small profits in very brief time frames. Unfortunately, the combined effect of these systems tends to erase trading opportunities faster than they can be identified with traditional charting tools. Trading platforms available to the general public—even those with sophisticated rules-based capabilities—are no match for these systems, which operate in the millisecond time frame.

The collaborative effort between IBM and TD Securities mentioned in the preceding chapter is a perfect example. The system is designed to process more than two million messages received from a variety of market sources in less than a second. The combination of large communication bandwidth and supercomputer processing speed allows such systems to identify trading patterns, make decisions, and place trades all within a time frame invisible to traditional charting techniques. Such systems are so fast that they are sensitive to very small propagation delays from the data sources. The problem has been solved, in part, by replacing electrical wires with fiber-optic links.

This new level of precision and speed has completely changed the game and given new meaning to the term "market efficiency." The implications are far-reaching because they raise important questions about the foundations of technical charting and analysis. Suppose, for example, that a specific combination of technical indicators is discovered that can reliably predict an impending large upward move of a stock price 70% of the time. The situation would represent a market inefficiency that, in the past, could have been exploited by an investor who detected the emerging trend as a chart pattern. Both independent and institutional traders have traditionally spent enormous amounts of time back testing various combinations of indicators and chart patterns to discover such anomalies. Not surprisingly, software platforms for active traders have evolved to support these activities.

Unfortunately, in the modern supercomputing era, algorithmic trading programs almost always detect and overexploit such inefficiencies, thereby extinguishing them. Both the chart pattern and its result disappear. The phenomenon can be illustrated in the following sequence, which tracks the trades of two competing institutions during a brief time frame spanning just a few seconds:

1. A reliable technical indicator gives a buy signal for a stock trading at $100.00.

2. Institution #1 buys 100,000 shares across several ticks $100.01-$100.05. Average purchase price = $100.03.

3. Institution #1 buys a second block of 100,000 shares across ticks $100.05-$100.15. Average purchase price = $100.10.

4. Institution #2 detects the trend and places a buy order as the stock ticks down to $100.08.

5. Institutions #1 and #2 each purchase 100,000 shares across ticks $100.08-$100.14. Average purchase price = $100.11.

6. Institution #1 stops buying; Institution #2 purchases 100,000 shares across ticks $100.14-$100.16. Average price = $100.15.

   Current Status:

   Institution #1 = 300,000 shares @ $100.08

   Institution #2 = 200,000 shares @ $100.13

7. Institution #1 sells 300,000 shares in multiple ticks (average selling price $100.14, profit = $0.06 × 300,000 shares = $18,000).

8. The chart pattern is disrupted and the uptrend ends as the stock begins falling.

9. Institution #2 (average price $100.13) begins selling aggressively as the price falls.

The first institutional investor was able to detect, exploit, and extinguish the emerging trend at the expense of the second institutional investor in addition to the public market. Similar logistics can be found in virtually any comparison of minute-by-minute and overlapping tick-by-tick data. Figure 2.1 illustrates these dynamics using a randomly selected two-minute trading interval for Apple Computer (ticker: AAPL) on 2009/04/24.

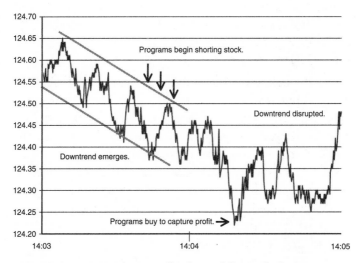

FIGURE 2.1   *Two-minute trading interval for Apple Computer (2009/04/24, 14:03-14:05). The interval included 995 separate ticks and a high-to-low price swing of $0.43. Despite the relatively large swing, the stock closed minute #2 only $0.09 below the opening price of minute #1.*

The stock opened minute #1 (14:03-14:04) trading at $124.58. A downtrend quickly emerged with successively lower highs and lower lows. The trend was evident to both sophisticated algorithmic trading systems and traditional charting programs. However, since algorithmic trading programs vary with regard to their ability to detect a trend, some programs would have initiated trades ahead of others. Furthermore, the broad market exhibited similar behavior, with the S&P 500 falling from 867.35 to 866.31 during minute #1. Complex programs tracking a large number of data streams from multiple markets would have also noticed that the euro briefly strengthened against the U.S. dollar during the previous three minutes (14:00-14:03), climbing from a low of 1.32424 to a high of 1.32621 before declining to 1.32540 during the minute ending at 14:04 (minute #1 of Figure 2.1). The sudden currency reversal is visible as a sharp spike on the 1-minute Euro:USD ratio chart.

At the beginning of minute #2, the price fell sharply. Algorithmic trading systems that closed their short positions near the bottom averaged more than $0.20 profit. This activity destroyed the downtrend by causing the stock to rise. It also caused the price to become more volatile. The chaos is evident throughout the minute. It became especially relevant near the end when the price suddenly spiked up into the original trading range of minute #1. Traders and programs that remained short lost all their profit during these few seconds.

The rise and fall pattern visible near the left side of Figure 2.1 was driven by the behavior of a large number of computer programs and private investors executing buy, sell, and sell short orders with different levels of aggressiveness at different times. Also included is the execution of previously entered stop/sell and stop/buy orders. Most sophisticated programs are designed to take advantage of these price swings by incrementally building positions across several up- and downticks.

In this particular case, the stock remained volatile for the remainder of the trading day. During the next two minutes it climbed to $124.52 before entering into a new downtrend that lasted for eight minutes. Beyond this point, the price climbed and fell sharply several times with no discernable pattern. Although the behavior appears to be random on charts displaying discreet time frames, tick-by-tick analysis reveals distinct trends that resemble those of Figure 2.1.

A key question emerges: If the actions of automated trading systems remove both the trend and its chart pattern, then why do trends lasting several minutes or longer exist at all? The answer lies in the fine structure of the individual tick-by-tick trading patterns. When the conditions that triggered the original trade persist, algorithmic trading systems will either keep the trades open or add to them. This activity itself often becomes an indicator that can trigger additional trades from other computerized systems and ultimately public customers. Alternatively, a trend can end because a single large trade achieves its profit goal and the responsible program begins unwinding the original trade. This activity can trigger a sharp reversal when other automated systems sense the change and also begin closing their positions.

Finally, moving from tick-by-tick analysis to bars composed of many ticks can create distortions that mask underlying volatility. These distortions can arise in any time frame that has precise boundaries. Charts built on single-minute bars are no more immune to the problem than charts built on bars depicting longer time frames because, as we saw in Figure 2.1, a single minute can contain multiple reversals. These changes and sub-trends are invisible at the level of granularity imposed by the length of each bar. If, for example, a chart is constructed using one-minute intervals, the exact timing of each minute's open and close determines whether a new trend appears orderly or disorderly. False trends often emerge under these circumstances that would not exist if the boundaries for each minute were shifted by just a few seconds.

A Simple Illustration

Financial markets are a zero-sum game in the sense that every dollar won by one investor must necessarily be lost by another. Competing against high-performance systems that trade at the individual tick level is, therefore, extraordinarily difficult for a public customer using standard off-the-shelf analytical tools. These concepts can be illustrated using a variety of scenarios that don't involve the stock market. Suppose, for example, that we were attempting to bet on the average length of a daily meeting scheduled to begin each day between 9:00 and 9:15 at a large corporation. For the purpose of this discussion, we will treat the meeting length as if it were a stock price. Earlier start times, therefore, translate into longer meetings. We will also assume that the same group of attendees is present at each meeting.

The scenario we will consider involves slight but steady decreases in the starting time of the meeting over the course of a few weeks. As with a stock price, changes in the meeting time display a certain level of volatility, and no trend is straight up or down. However, an astute investor charting the 10-day moving average has noticed a consistent pattern. Turning to a slightly more sophisticated analysis, he compares the 10- and 100-day moving averages and becomes convinced that a trend is emerging because the 10-day average has crossed below the 100-day average.

Many other charting tools and analytical approaches are available to our investor. Being cautious, he decides to look at broader trends that span several regular meeting schedules. A cursory review reveals that the starting times of several other morning meetings have also begun to fall, resulting in longer meetings. A strong upward trend is apparent across the company. Other dynamics support the trend: Starting time volatility is falling and attendance across all meetings is rising. In stock market terms these trends are interpreted as rising price (longer meetings), falling volatility (more consistent start time), and rising volume (more consistent attendance). If the meeting length were a stock price, our investor would go long by purchasing the stock or call options, or selling puts.

Unfortunately, all the evidence gathered by our investor is indirect. His institutional counterpart, however, has detailed real-time information that can be used to make precise predictions. This information is specific to each of the attendees. It includes the time they wake up, eat breakfast, leave their home, and whether they stop to put fuel in their car, in addition to details about the traffic they encounter on the way. Each data item arrives via a separate data feed, and the information is combined and processed to provide a constantly updated picture. Like the tick-by-tick systems used to predict trends in the stock market, this system is constructed with powerful computers and high-speed fiber-optic links.

Just as our first investor finalizes his decision to structure a long position, one of the data feeds reveals that a malfunctioning traffic light has caused a traffic jam that affects two of the meeting attendees. Only a few moments later, it is discovered that another attendee has stopped to buy fuel for her car. At this point in time, the computer program projects that the average arrival time will be five minutes later than that of the previous day. Armed with this information, the institutional investor takes the other side of the first investor's trade by shorting the stock, selling calls, or buying puts.

The institutional investor clearly wins this particular exchange by taking advantage of precise, timely, and detailed information. He has an undeniable advantage. Furthermore, the trend discovered by the first investor may be totally invalid. The only way to know would be to understand the combined effects of dozens of underlying parameters that affect the arrival times of the attendees. That information is available only to the second investor, who can best optimize his use of capital with very brief trades placed at just the right time.

Three key dynamics emerge from this discussion:

1. The first investor will always lose to the second regardless of the time frame.

2. Lengthening the time frame of the investment reduces the precision and increases the probability of being wrong.

3. The second investor agrees to accept a smaller per-trade profit in return for this precision. His strategy must then be to "chip away" at the market.

The high level of precision enjoyed by our second investor allows him to avoid the effects of volatility by remaining out of the market most of the time. Unlike the first investor, he can optimize the use of capital by moving money between different investments with no particular attachment to a single stock.

If the stock market is a gambling casino, our second investor is the house. Like the house, his strategy is to play with the odds in his favor and to use these odds to repeatedly capture small profits. The house rarely loses.

Testing the Market's Efficiency

We can verify that high-performance tick-by-tick trading extinguishes trends almost instantly by studying the statistics of single-minute price changes. A simple but crude test is to record the number of up minutes that are followed by another up minute, and the number of down minutes that are followed by another down minute. This test will serve as a launching point for our discussion, which will include increasingly selective filters and different time frames.

Table 2.1 describes the results of this first experiment. A single stock, Apple Computer (ticker: AAPL), was used because it is highly liquid and traded both by private investors and institutions. Results were compiled using 1 year (252 trading days) of minute-by-minute prices. The complete data set includes 98,085 individual minutes. The first column of the table contains threshold data for the first minute. In all cases, the second minute has no threshold.

TABLE 2.1   *Number of Minutes Repeating the Direction of a Previous Minute for 1 Year of Apple Computer Stock (The first column indicates the threshold used to filter the first minute. The data spans 98,085 trading minutes beginning on 2008/05/14 and ending on 2009/05/14.[1])*

Min#1 Change	Min#1 Up	Min#2 Up	Min#2 Down	Min#2 Same	Up-Up Avg.	Up-Down Avg.	Up-Same Avg.
0.000	47,543	22,178	23,818	1,547	0.466	0.501	0.033
0.001	18,925	8,707	9,743	475	0.460	0.515	0.025
0.002	7,143	3,286	3,710	147	0.460	0.519	0.021
0.003	3,116	1,433	1,634	49	0.460	0.524	0.016
0.004	1,552	703	827	22	0.453	0.533	0.014
0.005	826	363	453	10	0.439	0.548	0.012
0.006	469	207	258	4	0.441	0.550	0.009
0.007	291	128	160	3	0.440	0.550	0.010
0.008	176	74	100	2	0.420	0.568	0.011
0.009	115	53	61	1	0.461	0.530	0.009
0.010	80	42	37	1	0.525	0.463	0.013
0.011	47	26	20	1	0.553	0.426	0.021
0.012	30	18	11	1	0.600	0.367	0.033
0.013	23	15	8	0	0.652	0.348	0.000
0.014	17	11	6	0	0.647	0.353	0.000
0.015	15	9	6	0	0.600	0.400	0.000
0.016	8	5	3	0	0.625	0.375	0.000
0.017	6	3	3	0	0.500	0.500	0.000
0.018	6	3	3	0	0.500	0.500	0.000
0.019	6	3	3	0	0.500	0.500	0.000
0.020	6	3	3	0	0.500	0.500	0.000

No clear correlation emerges. This statement remains true all the way to the bottom of the table, where a severe first-minute change threshold of 2% reduces the number of events to just 6 (0.006% of the total number of minutes). Of these 6 events, 3 were followed by a second up minute. Whether this ratio is significant is debatable; in either case it is surprising that only 50% of the following minutes closed higher because these events are highly unusual. At a lower threshold of 1.5% the results are similar: 9 of the following minutes continued the trend. The slight increase to 60% is not statistically significant because the number of events is small.

The slight increase in trend-following minutes near the bottom of the table might also be caused by order imbalances and filled trading queues—situations that often take more than a single minute to resolve. Volume data supports this assertion. The average volume for these unusual minutes is 6.4× that of a typical minute (517,445 versus 80,965). Table 2.2 displays relevant data for each of the unusual minutes. Most of these large price changes can be traced to a single event.

For example, the large price changes of 2008/10/03 were related to spectacular news that rocked the financial markets. Unemployment jumped to 6.1% as employers reduced their payrolls by the largest amount in 5 years, and the U.S. Congress approved an unprecedented $700 billion economic bailout plan for financial institutions. Rumors and news flooded the markets throughout the day and the remainder of the week as the Dow fell from 10,484 at the open on 10/03 to 8,451 at the close on 10/10. Only one event on the list includes two consecutive changes larger than 1.5%: the 2008/10/09 spike spanning the minutes ending at 15:55 and 15:56. However, 2008/10/10 had 4 nonconsecutive minutes with very large price changes. On this particular day gold fell more than 6%; oil prices dropped $4.80 to a 1-year low; London's FTSE, the CAC in Paris, and the XETRA DAX in Germany each lost about 10% of their value during the first 10 minutes of trading; and officials from the Group of Seven (G7) countries issued a five-point plan aimed at reversing the worldwide credit crisis. The president of the United States also spoke publicly about the global financial crisis. Each event, news item, rumor, and analyst comment affected the market that day.

TABLE 2.2 *Minutes Displaying Close-to-Close Price Changes Larger Than 1.5% in Table 2.1*

Date	Closing Time	Prev. Close	Open	High	Low	Close	Volume
2008/06/13	937	165.44	165.41	168.34	165.31	168.12	771,859
2008/09/16	1417	137.65	137.37	139.87	137.14	139.78	53,697
2008/09/29	1351	101.48	101.47	104.67	101.44	104.55	591,339
2008/10/01	1345	108.68	108.71	111.66	108.68	111.57	261,823
2008/10/03	950	96.68	96.68	99.97	94.65	99.91	1,407,562
2008/10/03	954	97.21	97.18	103.17	97.13	101.91	1,903,500
2008/10/08	934	87.74	87.78	89.11	87.53	89.11	368,437
2008/10/08	938	88.26	88.26	89.60	88.10	89.60	392,788
2008/10/09	1555	87.47	87.47	88.84	87.43	88.79	266,378
2008/10/09	1556	88.79	88.78	90.29	88.77	90.27	376,420
2008/10/10	938	85.01	85.08	88.10	85.00	88.10	302,617
2008/10/10	941	88.50	88.50	91.60	88.42	91.51	253,854
2008/10/10	955	91.59	91.60	93.00	91.54	92.99	247,392
2008/10/10	1001	92.60	92.61	94.07	92.51	94.06	315,446
2008/10/24	935	91.58	91.62	93.20	91.11	93.00	248,570

Table 2.1 reveals a slight tendency for very large price changes to affect the minute that follows. For example, 15 of the 23 spikes larger than 1.3% (65.2%) persisted beyond the boundary of the first minute. In an efficient market, however, it is unlikely that momentum will develop into a persistent trend once order imbalances are resolved and the market regains its normal equilibrium. These dynamics are apparent in the data of Table 2.3, which displays closing prices for minute #3. For this analysis, the 6 cases where minute #2 does not exhibit an upward price movement have been eliminated. Each line of the table, therefore, displays a case where minute #1 closed more than 1.5% above the previous minute (minute #0), and the next minute (minute #2) also closed up. Increases of only $0.01 in minute #3 were not counted because they are less than the typical bid-ask spread of the stock.

TABLE 2.3   *Minutes Displaying Close-to-Close Price Changes Larger Than 1.5% That Are Also Followed by an Up Minute (See Table 2.1. Closing prices are displayed for the previous minute [Min#0] and the two following minutes [Min#2, Min#3]. The final column marks cases where the uptrend of minute #1 persists into minute #3. The two increases of only $0.01 are not counted because they are smaller than the bid-ask spread of the stock. Data spans 98,085 trading minutes of Apple Computer stock beginning on 2008/05/14 and ending on 2009/05/14.)*

Date	Min#1 Closing Time	Min#0	Min#1	Min#2	Min#3	Min#3 Up > $.01
2008/06/13	937	165.44	168.12	168.89	169.45	xx
2008/09/29	1351	101.48	104.55	105.40	106.64	xx
2008/10/03	954	97.21	101.91	102.89	103.75	xx
2008/10/08	938	88.26	89.60	89.84	90.68	xx
2008/10/09	1555	87.47	88.79	90.27	90.28	
2008/10/09	1556	88.79	90.27	90.28	89.47	
2008/10/10	938	85.01	88.10	88.65	88.50	
2008/10/10	1001	92.60	94.06	94.10	94.11	
2008/10/24	935	91.58	93.00	93.34	93.55	xx

It is apparent from the data in Table 2.3 that even the largest single-minute price changes did not result in persistent trends. The uptrend of minute #1 continued beyond minute #2 in only 5 of 9 cases. This result is significant in that it raises questions about the value of a variety of trend-following technical indicators. Table 2.4 displays 3-minute data across the complete range of thresholds. As before, the first column lists the change threshold for minute #1. The second column, labeled "Min#1-#2 Up Test," counts the number of events where minute #1 was up more than the threshold amount and minute #2 also closed higher. The three columns that follow contain data about the direction of the third minute—up, same, or down. Instances where minute #3 closed down represent reversals of the trend initiated during the first 2 minutes. The probabilities associated with these reversals are listed in the final column at the right side of the table.

TABLE 2.4   *Behavior of Minute #3 after an Uptrend Established During Minutes #1 and #2 (In each case, minute #1 must exceed the change threshold listed in column 1 and minute #2 must continue the uptrend by closing higher than minute #1. Data spans 98,085 trading minutes of Apple Computer stock beginning on 2008/05/14 and ending on 2009/05/14.)*

Min#1 Change	Min#1-#2 Up Test	Min#3 Up	Min#3 Same	Min#3 Down	Min#3 Down %
0.0%	22,105	10,121	707	11,277	0.510
0.1%	8,674	3,948	207	4,519	0.521
0.2%	3,274	1,480	67	1,727	0.527
0.3%	1,428	661	14	753	0.527
0.4%	700	335	6	359	0.513
0.5%	362	181	3	178	0.492
0.6%	206	95	1	110	0.534
0.7%	127	61	1	65	0.512
0.8%	74	39	0	35	0.473
0.9%	53	24	0	29	0.547
1.0%	42	21	0	21	0.500

The data reveals a very slight tendency for minute #3 to reverse the trend begun during the first 2 minutes. Although subtle, the trend is statistically significant because it is evident across the dataset and can be seen at the top of the table where the number of tested events is large.

Although it is difficult to draw specific quantitative conclusions about the tendency for reversal after the initial 2-minute price change, it is clear that there is no solid evidence of a continuing uptrend. Surprisingly, the rare events near the bottom of the table are still not powerful enough to initiate an uptrend that persists into minute #3. These events involve an initial spike larger than 1% and a continuation of the trend as measured by the close of minute #2.

For completeness, the inverse of Table 2.4 is presented in Table 2.5. As before, the first column lists the change threshold for minute #1. The second column, labeled "Min#1-#2 Down Test," counts the number of events where minute #1 was down more than the threshold amount and minute #2 also closed down. The three columns that follow contain data about the direction of the third minute—down, same, or up. As before, instances in which minute #3 closed up represent reversals of the trend initiated during the first 2 minutes. The probabilities associated with these reversals are listed in the final column at the right side of the table.

TABLE 2.5   *Behavior of Minute #3 after a Downtrend Established During Minutes #1 and #2 (In each case, minute #1 must exceed the change threshold listed in column 1 and minute #2 must continue the downtrend by closing lower than minute #1. Data spans 98,085 trading minutes of Apple Computer stock beginning on 2008/05/14 and ending on 2009/05/14.)*

Min#1 Change	Min#1-#2 Down Test	Min#3 Down	Min#3 Same	Min#3 Up	Min#3 Reversal
0.0%	21,524	9,772	635	11,117	0.516
0.1%	8,560	3,901	192	4,467	0.522
0.2%	3,274	1,479	62	1,733	0.529
0.3%	1,393	634	25	734	0.527
0.4%	671	304	9	358	0.534
0.5%	361	158	6	197	0.546
0.6%	211	101	3	107	0.507
0.7%	127	60	1	66	0.520
0.8%	84	40	1	43	0.512
0.9%	56	26	1	29	0.518
1.0%	34	15	1	18	0.529

The results mirror those of the 3-minute uptrend experiment, with the most significant results displaying a very slight tendency for a reversal in the third minute. As before, there is no hint that the 2-minute uptrend persists under any set of experimental conditions. However, we must rule out other possibilities before concluding that the recent price history of a stock does not encode information that can be used to predict the future direction. For example, it might be the case that large initial price changes are often followed by a slight correction before the emerging trend continues. Under those circumstances, minute #3 of Tables 2.4 and 2.5 might represent regression toward the mean—a phenomenon often mentioned by technical analysts.

We can test the hypothesis that emerging trends often contain a brief reversal that subsequently vanishes before the trend continues. In such instances a return to the trend would be apparent in the stock's closing price several minutes later. Results of such an experiment are depicted in Table 2.6.

TABLE 2.6   *Trend Test Spanning 10 Minutes (The minute #1 price change must exceed a threshold value, and minute #11 must close above the closing price of minute #1. Data spans 98,085 trading minutes of Apple Computer stock beginning on 2008/05/14 and ending on 2009/05/14.)*

Min#1 Threshold	Min#1 Up	Min#11 Up	Up-Up Avg.	Avg. Chng
0.0%	46,424	22,598	0.487	−0.01
0.1%	18,429	8,997	0.488	−0.02
0.2%	6,933	3,373	0.487	−0.02
0.3%	3,015	1,501	0.498	0.00
0.4%	1,500	761	0.507	0.02
0.5%	791	393	0.497	0.04
0.6%	451	233	0.517	0.06
0.7%	278	146	0.525	0.06
0.8%	169	86	0.509	0.03
0.9%	111	62	0.559	0.11
1.0%	77	44	0.571	0.16

As before, the first column contains threshold values for minute #1. The second column (Min#1 Up) records the number of minutes that close higher than the previous minute by an amount greater than the threshold. The third column records whether the uptrend persists for another 10 minutes. If minute #1 exceeds the threshold requirement and minute #11 closes higher than minute #1, the event is counted in column #3 (Min#11

Up). The fourth column (Up-Up Avg) records the percentage chance of minute #2 continuing the uptrend if minute #1 exceeds the threshold listed in the first column. The final column (Avg Chng) records the average price change between minute #2 and minute #1 when minute #1 exceeds the threshold.

The probability of an uptrend persisting for 10 minutes increases very slightly as the threshold requirement for the first minute is raised. Although the statistical significance of the trend becomes questionable near the bottom of the table where the number of events is very small, the effect is clearly detectable near the top where the number of observed events is much larger. For example, at a threshold of 0% (any upward price change), the probability of the uptrend persisting through minute #11 is 49%. That value rises steadily to 57% as the threshold is raised to 1.0%. At this level, we can expect a single minute to meet the criterion only once in three days (77 events per year). However, if the indicator is reliable, 57% would be significant, and a rules-based trading program could be used to generate a steady profit. A well-designed program continuously scanning a list of stocks could be expected to uncover several trading opportunities each day. This approach is the essence of "black box" trading where a computer program chips away at the market by leveraging a small statistical anomaly. To be valid, the statistic would have to be true across all stocks chosen for the scan list.

Unfortunately, most anomalies are too small to be exploited by a public customer. This one is no exception. The 57% probability associated with continuation of the emerging uptrend translates into an average price increase of just $0.16 at the close of minute #11. Furthermore, capturing the $0.16 requires instant action in terms of opening and closing trades. Trading commissions and bid-ask spreads further degrade the situation. It would be impossible for a public customer to realize any gain from this particular inefficiency. Furthermore, the events are closely clustered; 66 of 77 occurred during September-October 2008 in an unstable market triggered by a worldwide banking crisis. Exploiting such distortions requires constant monitoring to determine when they vanish, and losses tend to accumulate as the inefficiency begins to disappear.

An almost endless variety of experiments can be designed to test these concepts. Most are beyond the scope of this book, which is not intended as a reference on technical charting. However, some basic examples can help extend the present discussion. One approach sets a price change threshold for the first minute based on the recent high or low of the stock. If the minute closes above or below the threshold, the next minute is checked to see if the stock has continued moving in the same direction. The results of a representative experiment are displayed in Table 2.7. Each minute's close is measured against the high (low) of the previous 20 minutes. If it closes higher (lower) by the threshold amount, the next minute is also checked. Each line of the table records results for a different threshold. For example, the second line of the table reveals that 3,527 minutes closed 0.1% above the high of the previous 20 minutes. The following minute also closed higher 1,508 times. Dividing the two numbers gives an event probability of 42.8%. Reading across the table, we discover that 3,731 minutes closed more than 0.1% below the low of the previous 20 minutes, and that the downward direction was repeated by the next minute 1,595 times (42.7%).

TABLE 2.7 *Number of 22-Minute Events Where Minute #21 Closed Above (Below) the High (Low) of the Previous 20 Minutes by More Than the Threshold Amount, and Minute #22 Repeated the Direction (Data spans 98,085 trading minutes of Apple Computer stock beginning on 2008/05/14 and ending on 2009/05/14.)*

Min#1 Threshold	Min#1 Up	Min#2 Up	Up-Up Avg.	Min#1 Down	Min#2 Down	Down-Down Avg.
0.0%	9,805	4,315	0.440	9,688	4,197	0.433
0.1%	3,527	1,508	0.428	3,731	1,595	0.427
0.2%	1,254	520	0.415	1,417	588	0.415
0.3%	516	208	0.403	608	249	0.410
0.4%	254	105	0.413	307	113	0.368
0.5%	133	57	0.429	170	60	0.353
0.6%	68	27	0.397	100	33	0.330
0.7%	39	19	0.487	66	23	0.348
0.8%	22	10	0.455	44	17	0.386
0.9%	14	7	0.500	34	15	0.441
1.0%	7	3	0.429	24	10	0.417

For each threshold, the price change of the second minute appears not to follow the first. This dynamic holds true for even the most severe cases near the bottom of the table. As revealed in previous experiments, the market appears to be efficient enough to absorb news, respond with a large price change, and return to normal functioning within the time frame of a single minute. Moreover, there appears to be some tendency for large downward spikes to reverse. For example, the 170 events characterized by downward price changes greater than 0.5% have less than a 35% chance of persisting into the next minute.

If downward price spikes larger than 0.5% have a 65% chance of reversing during the next minute, this information could provide a valuable investment opportunity. Building out the right side of Table 2.7 with more detail is essential to this analysis. Table 2.8 contains the appropriate information.

TABLE 2.8   *Detailed Analysis for 22-Minute Events Where Minute #21 Closed Below the Low of the Previous 20 Minutes by More Than the Threshold Amount (Columns 3-5 reveal the number of times minute #22 closed down, the same, or up from minute #21 after the threshold was achieved by minute #21. Column 7 measures the average price change between the close of minute #21 and the close of minute #22 for all events that meet the initial threshold requirement. Data spans 98,085 trading minutes of Apple Computer stock beginning on 2008/05/14 and ending on 2009/05/14.)*

Min#1 Threshold	Min#1 Down	Min#2 Down	Min#2 Same	Min#2 Up	Down- Up Avg.	Avg. Change
0.0%	9,688	4,197	257	5,234	0.540	0.01
0.1%	3,731	1,595	84	2,052	0.550	0.01
0.2%	1,417	588	20	809	0.571	0.03
0.3%	608	249	5	354	0.582	0.04
0.4%	307	113	1	193	0.629	0.07
0.5%	170	60	0	110	0.647	0.06
0.6%	100	33	0	67	0.670	0.11
0.7%	66	23	0	43	0.652	0.13
0.8%	44	17	0	27	0.614	0.11
0.9%	34	15	0	19	0.559	0.07
1.0%	24	10	0	14	0.583	0.15

The slight trend apparent in Table 2.7 is reinforced by a steady increase in the average closing price of minute #22. The average close-to-close reversal increases from $0.01 at the lowest threshold level to $0.15 for the 24 large and rare events at the bottom of the table. Unfortunately, as before, the average price reversal of $0.15 is too small to be exploited by a public customer. This small regression toward the mean is not totally unexpected. Moreover, the subtle differences between the left and right sides of Table 2.7 may be caused by short selling behavior. Large downward spikes often cause short sellers to capture profit by closing their positions. In this regard, stocks with heavy short interest have a history of large upward price reversals also known as "short covering rallies." The $0.15 average price reversals most likely represent brief short covering rallies.

The more liquid a market is, the less likely it is to display inefficiencies. Foreign exchange markets are, by far, the most liquid because they trade around the clock with each minute characterized by extremely high volumes. It is not unusual for a heavily traded currency like the U.S. dollar, British pound, or Japanese yen to trade considerably more value in 1 hour than a large cap stock in an entire day. Most estimates place the size of the foreign exchange markets at more than $4 trillion each day, with most of the volume concentrated in just four currencies: euro, yen, pound sterling, and Swiss franc. Furthermore, foreign exchange markets are instantly affected by virtually every piece of news in the world because the underlying trading population is located everywhere and connected to every financial market. This instant response is extended to include transactions that would be considered "insider trading" in the stock market—there is no such thing as insider trading of a currency.

The dynamics of the forex markets underscore the meaning of the word *efficiency*. Although there is no single exchange, prices for a given currency remain synchronized to within a fraction of a penny. This synchronization is driven by thousands of financial institutions trading with each other on a moment-by-moment basis. The smallest price difference represents an arbitrage that is immediately extinguished by one of the thousands of computer programs monitoring and trading the markets. Despite the huge trading population, tremendous liquidity, and computer-driven instantaneous execution, many individual investors still believe they can find a statistical edge using standard off-the-shelf charting software. Although it is certainly possible to use economic knowledge to make intelligent long-term predictions, and to successfully combine this knowledge with trading dynamics depicted in various charts, the idea of finding a market inefficiency that can be profitably traded is outdated.

This high level of efficiency is apparent in Table 2.9, which displays the number of minutes repeating the direction of a previous minute for one year of the U.S. dollar/yen pair (USD/JPY).[2]

TABLE 2.9 *Number of Minutes Repeating the Direction of a Previous Minute for One Year of USD/JPY (The first column indicates the threshold used to filter minute #1 changes. Values are absolute [e.g., the change from 103.672 to 103.683 is equal to 0.011]. Columns 3-5 reveal the number of times minute #2 closed up, down, or the same as minute #1. Columns 6-8 restate the values in columns 3-5 in percentage terms. The data spans 365,320 trading minutes beginning on 2008/04/24 and ending on 2009/04/23.)*

Min#1 Change	Min#1 Up	Min#2 Up	Min#2 Down	Min#2 Same	Up-Up Avg.	Up-Down Avg.	Up-Same Avg.
0.000	166,608	76,244	80,583	9,781	0.458	0.484	0.059
0.020	57,008	25,710	29,350	1,948	0.451	0.515	0.034
0.040	21,829	9,505	11,831	493	0.435	0.542	0.023
0.060	9,395	3,988	5,253	154	0.424	0.559	0.016
0.080	4,234	1,792	2,389	53	0.423	0.564	0.013
0.100	2,292	987	1,290	15	0.431	0.563	0.007
0.120	1,282	547	728	7	0.427	0.568	0.005
0.140	793	332	456	5	0.419	0.575	0.006
0.160	527	228	296	3	0.433	0.562	0.006
0.180	338	146	192	0	0.432	0.568	0.000
0.200	220	97	123	0	0.441	0.559	0.000

The data suggests a tendency for minute #2 to reverse the direction established in minute #1. As we have seen, such reversals, which normally represent regression toward the mean, are common distortions that cannot normally be traded. As in the Apple Computer stock example, these reversals are too small to generate profit for a public customer. Even the most extreme example at the bottom of the table—an event that occurs only 220 times out of 365,320—is too small to trade. Specific details are presented in Table 2.10, which extends Table 2.9 with average price change information at each

threshold level. The data reveals that the average downward price change for these 220 outsized spikes is only
0.0177 USD/JPY. At more than 100 yen per dollar, this
change represents less than 2/100 of a penny.

TABLE 2.10   *Average Change in Minute #2 Following a Minute #1
Upward Price Spike for USD/JPY (Thresholds for minute #1 are
listed in column 1; number of events where minute #1 exceeds the
threshold are listed in column 2; number of events where minute #2
reverses the trend are listed in column 3; values from column 3 are
restated in percentage terms in column 4; average minute #2 price
change for all events where minute #1 exceeds the threshold are listed
in column 5. The data spans 365,320 trading minutes beginning on
2008/04/24 and ending on 2009/04/23.)*

Min#1 Change	Min#1 Up	Min#2 Down	Up-Down Avg.	Up-Down Avg. Chng.
0.000	166,608	80,583	0.484	0.0002
0.020	57,008	29,350	0.515	−0.0007
0.040	21,829	11,831	0.542	−0.0023
0.060	9,395	5,253	0.559	−0.0039
0.080	4,234	2,389	0.564	−0.0048
0.100	2,292	1,290	0.563	−0.0051
0.120	1,282	728	0.568	−0.0070
0.140	793	456	0.575	−0.0086
0.160	527	296	0.562	−0.0117
0.180	338	192	0.568	−0.0133
0.200	220	123	0.559	−0.0177

Although subtle, the tendency for the USD/JPY ratio
to reverse during minute #2 increases slightly as the
minute #1 threshold level is increased (as the ratio falls,
the yen strengthens against the U.S. dollar). Near the
top of the table, the average price change for minute #2
is insignificant. At the bottom of the table, the change is
measurable but too small to be helpful to most private

investors. Because the currency markets are extremely efficient and price changes are small, traders often use high levels of leverage—often as much as 100 times their actual capital. This practice allows an investor with $100,000 to exploit small price changes by trading $10 million. However, in percentage terms the distortion is too small to exploit regardless of the circumstances.

As we have seen, reliable indicators and persistent trends often appear in situations where execution logistics, timing, or trading costs make it impossible to exploit the inefficiency. For stocks, these dynamics are often found at the tick level, where they cannot be extinguished by normal market forces. An example using 60,000 ticks of Apple Computer stock is displayed in Table 2.11. As before, each line represents data for a different threshold. For clarity, because this analysis counts individual ticks as small as a single penny, the threshold is measured as a change greater than or equal to the value in column 1 (e.g., the first line sets a threshold for the next price change as greater than or equal to $0.01). Since $0.01 is the smallest possible price change for a stock, the threshold listed in line 1 maintains its previous meaning as "any change."

TABLE 2.11   *Percentage Chance of a Single Tick Price Change Repeating the Direction of the Previous Change for 60,000 Ticks of Apple Computer Stock on 2009/04/24 (Data spans the time frame from 12:38 to 16:00. The first column indicates the threshold used to filter the first tick [values in $0.01]. Note: threshold is measured as >= the value in column 1.)*

Tick#1 Change	Tick#1 Up	Tick#2 Up	Up-Up Avg.	Tick#1 Down	Tick#2 Down	Down-Down Avg.
0.010	12,100	4,164	0.344	12,187	4,251	0.349
0.020	9,497	3,212	0.338	9,568	3,302	0.345
0.030	2,921	865	0.296	2,864	893	0.312
0.040	2,037	592	0.291	2,026	604	0.298
0.050	716	194	0.271	711	193	0.271
0.060	274	75	0.274	285	76	0.267
0.070	216	57	0.264	214	60	0.280
0.080	123	34	0.276	120	28	0.233
0.090	69	16	0.232	65	17	0.262
0.100	54	13	0.241	49	13	0.265
0.110	25	6	0.240	30	6	0.200

Because each tick is an individual transaction, many ticks can occur at the same price. Transactions occurring at the same price are referred to as zero plus or zero minus ticks. A zero plus tick occurs when the execution price is the same as the previous transaction, but greater than the most recent trade at a different price. For example, if a series of trades execute at $50.01, $50.05, and $50.05, the last trade is the zero plus tick because it executed at the same price as the previous transaction, but higher than the preceding tick of $50.01. A zero minus tick is the reverse—the execution price remains the same as the last trade, but lower than the most recent trade at a different price.

The zero plus/zero minus effect is enhanced by programs that split trades into many smaller pieces. Institutional traders often use such programs to disguise very large transactions that can affect the market they are attempting to trade in. For example, a trade to sell 10,000 shares of a stock at $50 is often entered into the queue as 100 trades of 100 shares at a price of $50. These trades will ultimately generate 100 identically priced ticks or transactions. It is also common for the trading queue to contain many different sets of trades that can be matched off at the same price. As these trades execute, multiple ticks are recorded at that price. The result is a flat spot on the tick-by-tick chart.

Because our goal is to study the impact of one price change on the next, zero plus and zero minus ticks were removed from the data analyzed in Table 2.11. For example, line 6 of the table should be interpreted to mean that the stock experienced 274 upticks greater than or equal to $0.06, and that the next price change continued in the same direction only 75 times (27.4%). Conversely, the next price change was a downtick 72.6% of the time.

The data reveals a tendency for large price changes to trigger an immediate reversal. At the extreme end of the spectrum where only 25 price changes exceed the threshold, the probability of the next tick continuing in the same direction is only 24%. Furthermore, unlike in previous tables that were constructed on 1-minute boundaries, the tick results have very little noise. This consistency is visible in Figure 2.2, which charts the relationship between the number of primary upticks exceeding each threshold and the number of secondary price changes that follow in the same direction.

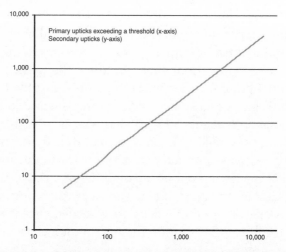

FIGURE 2.2   *Log-log plot of the number of upticks exceeding various predetermined thresholds (x-axis) versus the number of repeat upticks (y-axis). Using log scales for both axes allows the display of a large range of values.*

At the left side of the graph where the threshold is high, 25 primary upticks are followed by only 6 secondary upticks (24.0%). At the right side of the chart no threshold is applied, and 12,100 primary upticks are followed by 4,164 secondary price changes in the same direction (34.4%). The ratio shrinks at a steady predictable rate that yields a nearly perfect line with constant slope in the log-log plot. This consistency results from a lack of timing boundaries between the price changes, and the market's inability to erase the trend.

These results have significant meaning because they uncover a region of very brief time frames and very small price changes where persistent trends cannot be erased by the market. This region of the very brief and very small has become the new target for large financial institutions armed with the most powerful computers and software.

Fooled by Randomness

Automated trading can take many forms. Fully computerized trading at the tick level lies at one end of a spectrum that also includes private investors who manually place trades based on chart patterns. However, as more brokers offer their customers access to customizable rules-based trading systems, the practice of observing chart patterns and manually placing trades is likely to disappear.

Identifying a reliable set of technical indicators is only the first step in the process of creating a trading system. The next, and most important, step involves defining specific rules for entering and exiting trades. Most often, these rules are based on a combination of risk tolerance and technical indicators. Many investors make the mistake of defining rules for entering a trade and simply exit when they have a profit or begin losing money. They purchase a stock based on the appearance of a chart pattern with the hope of achieving a certain percentage gain. If the stock moves against them, and the trade loses more than a predefined amount, they stop out.

More sophisticated systems rely on specific indicators for both entering and exiting a trade. A common example involves tracking two moving averages of different length. A long position is initiated when the short-term moving average crosses from below to above the long-term average. The same position is closed at a later time when the short-term average once again crosses the long-term average in the opposite direction—that is, the short-term average falls from above to below the long-term average.

Figure 2.3 displays the results of an unusual test—the stock chart being analyzed was created by a random number generator. Each point on the chart was created by adding a random number to the value of the previous point.[3] The gray line traces the stock price across 510 trading days; the heavy dashed line follows the 50-day moving average; and the light dashed line follows the 20-day moving average.

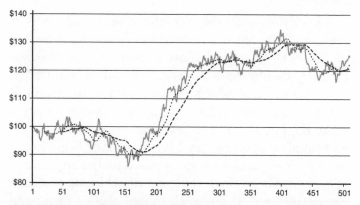

FIGURE 2.3   *Randomly generated daily stock chart with two moving averages—short-term (20 closes) and long-term (50 closes). The gray line traces the stock price across 510 trading days. Each of the moving averages is displayed using a dashed line. The heavy dashed line displays the long-term moving average, the light dashed line displays the short-term moving average. Price is displayed on the y-axis, and closes are counted on the x-axis.*

Each time the short-term (fast) moving average crosses the long-term (slow) average, a trade is opened or closed. The only exception is the final trade at the right side of the chart. A buy signal appeared on day 504 with the stock trading at 123.70. At the edge of the chart, with the stock trading at $125.19, a sell signal had not yet appeared. We have two choices regarding the open trade: We can close the trade for a small profit at the final price on the chart ($125.19), or we can eliminate the trade from our analysis. Closing the trade at the last price on the chart yields an overall profit of $23.07 (23.9%). Eliminating the incomplete trade results in a slightly lower gain of $21.58 (22.4%). Either approach reveals a very profitable trading strategy across 2 trading years. Moreover, the gain was achieved with only 6 trades. Table 2.12 outlines the results for each entry-exit pair.

TABLE 2.12   *Buy and Sell Data for Figure 2.3*

Buy Day	Buy ($)	Sell Day	Sell ($)	Gain/Loss ($)
115	96.40	129	94.43	−1.98
180	96.04	316	123.21	27.17
323	126.44	335	118.60	−7.84
359	125.94	419	127.74	1.80
486	119.86	496	121.30	1.43
497	121.92	503	122.91	0.99
504	123.70	510	125.19	1.49
		Gain		$23.07
		Gain %		23.9%

The largest gain occurred when the fast-moving average remained continually above the slow-moving average during the 136-day rise from $96.04 to $123.21. The trading strategy worked well during this time frame because it kept the trade open despite small but brief drawdowns. It also functioned well by closing a trade on day 419 just before a $10.00 drop in the price. These successes were partially offset by the failure to immediately close the trade initiated on day 323 as the stock rapidly fell nearly $6.00.

All factors considered, the strategy—despite its simplicity—seemed to function well and deliver an excellent return. Unfortunately, the stock being analyzed is not real. This situation raises important questions because we were able to successfully back test the indicator across a fairly long (2-year) period of time. More surprising is the stocklike appearance of the random chart. This phenomenon has been noted by previous authors—most notably Benoit Mandelbrot in his book *The (Mis)behavior of Markets*. In his discussion of fractals, Mandelbrot points out that "chance can produce deceptively convincing patterns."[4]

Both the chart and the lengths of the moving averages were randomly chosen. However, not every chart generates a strong positive return. Some are decidedly negative. Both extremes are surprising. The discussion raises a second question related to "over fitting." We can further enhance the return of Figure 2.3 by altering the length of each of the moving averages. Moreover, a set of high-yielding technical indicators can be selected for any chart—random or real. Modern back testing programs with optimization functions further enhance this problem when they are overused by investors.

Figure 2.4 and Table 2.13 were designed to illustrate this point with a slightly more sophisticated example. As before, the stock chart was created by a random number generator. Entry points for purchasing stock occur when the stock crosses the 50-day moving average in the positive direction. An exit point occurs when the stock falls more than 2.5% below the high of the 10 most recent closes. Additionally, new long trades are not initiated if an entry point occurs with the stock trading more than 2.5% below the 10-day high. This additional parameter is important because it prevents the system from entering a new long position on an uptick that occurs during a steep decline. Stated differently, the trigger conditions require that the stock be trading within 2.5% of the recent high when it crosses the 50-day moving average.

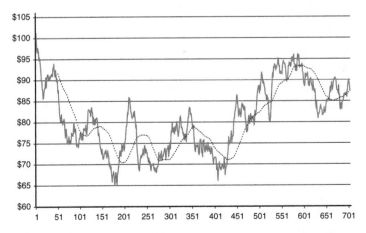

FIGURE 2.4   *Randomly generated daily stock chart overlaid with the 50 close moving average. The gray line traces the stock price; the dashed line displays the 50 close moving average. Price is displayed on the y-axis, and closes are counted on the x-axis.*

TABLE 2.13   *Buy and Sell Data for Figure 2.4*

Buy Day	Buy ($)	Sell Day	Sell ($)	Gain/Loss ($)
107	77.44	114	77.29	–0.15
189	72.95	213	83.62	10.67
276	72.81	283	70.91	–1.90
284	71.43	292	71.06	–0.37
293	72.52	298	71.82	–0.70
336	77.21	337	75.44	–1.77
338	77.68	349	80.73	3.05
428	71.60	438	75.10	3.50
479	81.20	488	79.30	–1.90
490	82.71	508	89.20	6.49
527	85.97	546	91.63	5.66
585	95.04	590	93.00	–2.04
655	85.60	674	87.55	1.95
690	86.54	703	87.29	0.75
		Gain		$23.24
		Gain%		30.0%

The rules performed exceptionally well during the most volatile time frames by rapidly stopping out of new trades and limiting losses. Days 276-298 are an excellent example. Despite several price reversals that generated false entry signals, losses were held to just $2.97. We could further tune the rules to accommodate more volatile stocks by reducing the 2.5% retracement threshold for exiting trades. However, reducing this threshold can also cause the system to prematurely exit an uptrend when the stock experiences a brief correction. One way to compensate for this problem is to generate more entry signals by reducing the length of the moving average. In this example, reducing the length from 50 to 20 days more than doubles the number of new trades from 14 to 30. Optimizing the trading rules is a complex multivariable problem.

The realization that we can tune a set of indicators and trading rules to a random stock chart and ultimately create a system that delivers outstanding profits is disturbing. It also demonstrates the importance of strictly following a set of rules. Both examples generated positive returns because they included a methodology for quickly closing losing trades. Staying in trades that continue to generate profit and closing trades that move in the wrong direction can improve the chances of generating a profit—even when the underlying price changes are totally random. Such systems can make it difficult to distinguish between real and randomly generated price change data.

Insider Trading

Most books on investing never mention insider trading. However, illegal or not, insider trading has become a distorting force in the equity markets and it should not be ignored. Moreover, it is often possible to detect distortions in the options market that hint at the behavior of insiders. These distortions can often be exploited for profit.

The academic research community has studied this phenomenon extensively. The work has produced a considerable amount of evidence pointing to highly profitable option trades that are often executed with a level of precision that cannot be explained as normal trading behavior. In many cases, "smart" traders sell options to the market that become worthless after key events such as earnings releases. They also seem to have the uncanny ability, just before an event, to purchase far out-of-the-money options that multiply many times in value. Some of the most notorious examples occurred just before the September 11, 2001 terrorist attacks when put contract volumes soared for American and United Airlines, residents of the World Trade Center (Morgan Stanley), and reinsurance companies. The German Central Bank President, Ernst Welteke, later reported, "There are ever clearer signs that there were activities on international financial markets that must have been carried out with the necessary expert knowledge." Insider trading before the 9/11 attacks was not confined to stocks. The markets also saw surges in gold, oil, and 5-year U.S. Treasury notes—each considered to be a solid investment in the event of a world crisis. In this regard it is also important to remember that the term "insider trading" applies to some, but not all, financial instruments. The term has no meaning, for example, in the context of currency trading, or for investments in commodities like gold and oil.

Much of the data used to support these assertions can be obtained from the Options Clearing Corporation (OCC) of the Chicago Board Options Exchange. The OCC data provides summary statistics for public customer trades based on order size: fewer than 100 contracts, 101-200 contracts, and more than 200 contracts. OCC suggests classifying trades larger than 200 contracts as institutional. Most academic research has focused on the behavior of institutional customers, those trading hundreds or thousands of contracts.

The difference between institutional and private investors becomes most apparent in the case of expensive stocks because the collateral requirement becomes prohibitive for large contract sizes. Google stock is an excellent example. At the time of this writing, the stock traded for more than $400 per share. Selling 1,000 at-the-money put or call options would, therefore, require an investor to have more than $10 million of collateral in their brokerage account. Worse still, if the contracts were exercised, more than $40 million would be needed to execute the trade. It can be reasonably assumed that large sellers tend to be institutional traders, and that private investors tend to be buyers or small-volume sellers. These differences have been exploited by researchers to pinpoint the sources of high-precision successful trades.

Significant insider activity can also occur among private investors. A classic example that strongly impacted the options market occurred in June 1995 when IBM purchased Lotus Development Corporation. On Thursday June 1, Lotus stock closed at $29.25 but the volume of out-of-the-money $40 strike price calls had risen from nearly zero to more than 400 contracts for no apparent reason. The trend continued on Friday with the stock closing at $30.50 and 416 of the $40 calls trading for $3/16 (just over $0.18). On Monday June 5, the stock closed at $32.50 and the volume of the $40 calls jumped to 1,043 contracts at $9/16 ($0.56). The next day, after the acquisition was announced, the stock closed at $61.43 and the $40 strike price calls traded for $21.75—a 3800% profit. The $58,000 invested in these options the previous day was now worth nearly $2.3 million. Someone knew something and it was reflected in active trading of deep out-of-the-money, nearly worthless calls.[5]

Similar behavior among private investors was observed just prior to IBM's November 2007 announcement of its acquisition of Cognos—a business intelligence software company. On Thursday November 8 with the NASDAQ 100 sharply down 2.92%, Cognos stock defied the market by rising 4.1%. The trend continued the next day. In total, the stock climbed 7.6% during the 2 days preceding the announcement while the rest of the tech market fell sharply (the NASDAQ 100 was down another 3.41% on Friday November 9). IBM announced the acquisition on Monday morning, and the stock jumped another 7.9%.[6,7]

We will return to a discussion of insider trading in the context of specific events such as earnings announcements, timed releases of economic indicators, and surprise news announcements.

Summary

During the past few years, financial markets have become enormously efficient. The trend has been driven by both private investors with advanced trading platforms, and large institutions with high-performance computing platforms. Ten years ago, private investors lacked access to real-time trading platforms or analytical tools. Software for creating stock charts was crude at best, and historical data was difficult to find.

The Internet created an environment that allowed brokers to offer their customers comprehensive trading platforms with real-time charting and analytical tools.

These platforms have evolved and now include flexible scripting languages for creating new indicators, access to tick-by-tick data, and rules-based automated trading.

Large institutions have also evolved their trading platforms. The newest versions are built around very high-performance computers capable of processing millions of pieces of financial information per second. Supporting these efforts are high-speed data links that bring together information from different financial markets. These systems facilitate trading at the tick level, where subtle inefficiencies allow the repeated capture of very small profits in very brief time frames.

Unfortunately, the combined efforts of institutional traders equipped with supercomputing platforms and millions of sophisticated private investors with real-time access to financial markets and news has created a situation where inefficiencies are extinguished almost immediately. As a result, it has become nearly impossible to find a combination of pricing parameters or chart patterns that can be profitably exploited for any length of time. In today's markets, inefficiencies persist only at the tick level, where private investors cannot react quickly enough to exploit them, and the profit from each trade is vanishingly small. At the institutional level, the game has changed to one of discovering inefficiencies first and exploiting them as long as possible until they disappear. The war is fought between rival computer systems, with speed and precision being the most important considerations.

Many of these problems are disguised by back testing systems that allow traders to overoptimize a set of technical indicators and rules. This problem is routinely referred to as "over fitting." By selecting the right set of parameters, it is even possible to create a set of rules that yield strong positive returns against randomly generated stock charts.

In the next chapter we will examine strategies for taking advantage of subtle distortions and anomalies in option prices. These distortions can form a reliable basis for many types of trades because they don't require an investor to predict the direction of the underlying financial instrument. As such, they provide statistical advantages that cannot be extinguished by the market as simple inefficiencies.

Further Reading

M. Carhart, R. Kaniel, D. K. Musto, and A. V. Reed, "Leaning for the Tape: Evidence of Gaming Behavior in Equity Mutual Funds," *Journal of Finance* 57, no. 2 (April 2002): 661-693.

P. Hillion and P. Suominen, "The Manipulation of Closing Prices," *Journal of Financial Markets* 7 (2004): 351-375.

K. John and L. Lang, "Strategic Insider Trading Around Dividend Announcements: Theory and Evidence," *Journal of Finance* 46 (1991): 1361-1398.

J. W. Liu, "Has Google Stock Price Been Manipulated?" SSRN eLibrary, February 4, 2009, http://ssrn.com/paper=1337350.

Julia Sawicki and K. Shrestha, "Insider Trading and Earnings Management," *Journal of Business Finance & Accounting* 35, no. 3-4 (April 2008): 331-346.

Wen Yu and Robert J. Bricker, "Earnings Valuation and Insider Trading," SSRN eLibrary, September 18, 2008, http://ssrn.com/paper=1014252.

Endnotes

1. Opening minutes are not used in this analysis because, in each case, the previous trading minute occurred 17 hours earlier at the previous day's close.

2. Foreign Exchange is a 24-hour market. It opens Sunday at 17:00 EST and closes Friday at 16:00 EST. To avoid distortions, the opening minute after each weekend is not included in this analysis.

3. Random numbers between –2.0 and +2.0 were generated in an Excel spreadsheet macro. Widening the range of the numbers simulates higher volatility or longer intervals between closes; narrowing the range simulates lower volatility or shorter intervals.

4. Benoit Mandelbrot and R. L. Hudson, *The (Mis)behavior of Markets* (New York: Basic Books—a member of The Perseus Books Group, 2004).

5. Stocks and options were priced in increments of 1/16 (6.25 cents).

6. E. Savitz, "What's Up With Cognos?" *Barrons—Tech Trader Daily,* November 8, 2007.

7. E. Savitz, "Well, That Would Explain It: IBM to Buy Cognos," *Barrons—Tech Trader Daily,* November 12, 2007.

Chapter 3

Trading Volatility Distortions

Key Concepts

- Institutional investors often build complex three-dimensional maps that relate implied volatility to calendar information and price of the underlying security.

- Distortions and anomalies in these maps represent trading opportunities in the form of mispriced volatility.

- Overnight (close-to-open), intraday (open-to-close), and traditional (close-to-close) measures of volatility can vary dramatically. These differences can be used to identify mispriced options and structure statistically advantaged trades.

- Volatility distortions sometimes vary by weekday. These calendar effects can help time entry and exit points for certain types of short-term trades.

Introduction—The Implied
Volatility Surface

It is important to distinguish between the fair value of an option and its exchange traded price. Contemporary pricing models, and in particular the Black-Scholes formula, are designed to calculate a fair price based on the amount of time left before expiration, underlying stock price, risk-free interest rate, and volatility. All but one of these parameters—volatility—can be precisely determined. The problem is one of change. Prices are dynamic, and it is very unusual for the underlying volatility of any financial instrument to remain constant over time. Stocks respond to world events, rumors, analyst comments, company news, and general market conditions. Volatility swings, therefore, are the norm not the exception.

However, it is important to estimate historical volatility so that the trading price of an option can be compared to its theoretical value. When an option is heavily traded, it can be assumed that market forces will push the price close to the correct theoretical value. In effect, the market is voting on the price through hundreds, or sometimes thousands, of trades. Surprisingly, this price is often very different from the value obtained by calculating the recent historical volatility of the stock.

Institutional investors often build complex three-dimensional maps that relate implied volatility to calendar information and price of the underlying security. These maps, or volatility surfaces as they are commonly known, are an important tool for determining the fair value of an option. Over time the maps accumulate and form a library of surfaces that can be used to analyze specific market conditions. For example, a three-dimensional map can be constructed with strike prices on the x-axis, term to expiration on the y-axis, and implied volatility on the z-axis (vertical axis). The map would be specific to a particular date and set of market conditions. At a later date when the market and, more important, the individual security display similar characteristics, the map can be retrieved for comparison to actual trading prices. These maps often reveal repeating oscillations—stochastics—that can be used to predict rising and falling implied volatility.

None of this work would be possible if contemporary option pricing theories were completely correct because the map would be flat. In a perfect world where price changes are random and returns fit a normal distribution, implied volatility would be constant across strike prices and expiration months; there would be no three-dimensional surface to discuss. Exactly the opposite is true. Sophisticated option traders who use the Black-Scholes formula in their option pricing models must continuously adjust their volatility assumptions to arrive at the actual trading price of an option. These adjustments are necessary because different expiration-strike combinations can be expected to have different implied volatilities.

Figure 3.1 displays an implied volatility surface for call options on the CBOE Volatility Index (ticker: VIX) on 2009/05/27 with the index at 32.36. The VIX was chosen for this illustration because it has one of the most interesting surfaces with regard to differences between months and strike prices. The figure reveals a steep skew between individual strikes superimposed on overall declining volatility from month to month. The steep skew is visualized as declining implied volatility from left to right; month-to-month changes at a particular strike, also referred to as term structure, are visible from front to back (depth axis). The chart reveals a flattening of the volatility skew over time. In June the values range from 86% to 143%. By November the range has compressed to 38% to 67%. The combined effects of these changes creates a characteristic shape that can be used to rapidly spot distortions in the form of hills, valleys, or flat spots. Institutional traders structure their trades around these distortions when they believe the market will erase them. Such decisions can be reinforced by comparing the current surface to previous versions for the same stock or index.

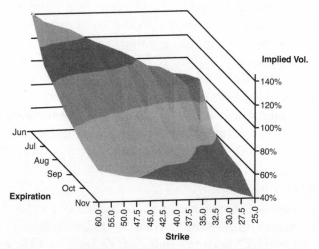

FIGURE 3.1   *Implied volatility surface for CBOE Volatility Index (ticker: VIX) call options on 2009/05/27 with the index at 32.36. Strike prices appear on the horizontal axis, expiration months on the depth axis, and implied volatility on the vertical axis. The number of days remaining before expiration: June, 20; July, 55; August, 83; September, 111; October, 146; November, 174.[1]*

Chapter 1, "Basic Concepts," discussed one of the most basic components of the volatility surface: the implied volatility skew, or "smile." This particular distortion, which was designed to accommodate the risk of a rapid price collapse, causes lower strikes to be priced with higher implied volatility. As a result, out-of-the-money puts are relatively more expensive than in-the-money puts, and in-the-money calls are less expensive than out-of-the-money calls. An implied volatility surface is, in effect, a visual representation of a series of monthly skews. The image displayed in Figure 3.1 appears as the inverse of a typical surface because higher strikes have higher implied volatility—that is, the skew appears to run backward. This inversion makes sense because the VIX tends to rise when the market falls. An investor who expects the market to fall might, therefore, purchase VIX calls or sell VIX puts.

Implied volatility surfaces are excellent tools for any options trader because they contain a tremendous amount of information. For example, they can be especially valuable to an investor who needs to select the best combination of options for a calendar spread because they offer insight into differences between various expiration/strike combinations. At the other end of the spectrum, institutional investors use automated systems to rapidly compare thousands of profiles, and to model the evolution of a surface as time progresses.

Implied volatility surfaces are relatively easy to create. Figure 3.1 was generated in just a few minutes using values displayed in an option pricing table and Excel's charting tool. The image was reduced from color to grayscale for publication purposes. Actual values for the chart are displayed in Table 3.1.

TABLE 3.1   *Values Used to Create the Implied Volatility Surface Displayed in Figure 3.1*

Strike	Jun	Jul	Aug	Sep	Oct	Nov
25.0	0.86	0.94	0.62	0.54	0.52	0.38
27.5	0.87	0.89	0.67	0.59	0.55	0.43
30.0	0.93	0.89	0.68	0.59	0.56	0.48
32.5	0.94	0.88	0.70	0.62	0.58	0.50
35.0	1.01	0.90	0.71	0.64	0.60	0.53
37.5	1.07	0.90	0.75	0.66	0.61	0.55
40.0	1.11	0.93	0.77	0.68	0.61	0.56
42.5	1.15	0.94	0.81	0.69	0.63	0.57
45.0	1.21	0.96	0.82	0.70	0.64	0.59
47.5	1.27	0.97	0.84	0.72	0.65	0.60
50.0	1.30	1.00	0.86	0.74	0.67	0.62
55.0	1.34	1.03	0.91	0.78	0.70	0.64
60.0	1.43	1.07	0.94	0.81	0.72	0.67

The implied volatility surface for VIX options displays unusually large differences between strike prices and months. The VIX is unusual because it represents the implied volatility priced into options on S&P 500 stocks. Volatility of the VIX, therefore, is best thought of as the volatility of volatility.

Stocks and indexes display profiles with much flatter skews and term structure. Figure 3.2 displays an implied volatility surface for call options on the SPDR Trust exchange traded fund (ticker: SPY), which closely mirrors the minute-by-minute behavior of the S&P 500. The steepest skew occurs in the fourth month and implied volatility is consistently depressed in the second month (visible as a rift in the chart). This rift is the most consistent and visible feature. Option traders sometimes structure positions that take advantage of such a distortion.

In this case, the simplest example involves a calendar spread that is short a June call and long a July call. This position would take advantage of the apparent underpricing of July options in addition to accelerating time decay of June options as expiration approaches. It is most appropriate for a bullish investor who expects the market to rise.

Overall, the differences are much more subtle than in the previous example. Data for the figure spans June through July because October options had not begun trading when the chart was created.

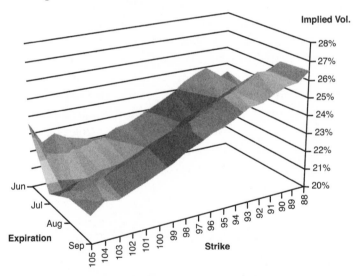

FIGURE 3.2   *Implied volatility surface for the SPDR Trust (ticker: SPY), which mirrors the performance of the S&P 500 index. Values were collected at the market close on 2009/06/01 with SPY trading at $94.43. Expiration months appear on the depth axis, strike prices on the horizontal axis, and implied volatility on the vertical axis. The number of days remaining before expiration: June, 19; July, 47; August, 82; September, 110.[2]*

Because implied volatility priced into options can differ significantly from actual volatility of the underlying stock or index, it is important to have access to both sets of information. Both pictures are complex: Implied volatility varies between strikes and expirations; historical volatility varies with the length of the window used for its calculation. As discussed in the next section, volatility can also vary significantly from one time of day to another. For example, as one might expect, volatility from close to open (overnight) tends to be smaller than from open to close (intraday). Certain days are also more volatile—most notably, days that include scheduled announcements such as earnings. One of the best examples of this phenomenon occurs when the Weekly Petroleum Status Report is released by the Energy Information Agency each Wednesday at 10:30. Stocks and exchange traded funds that are closely linked to the price of oil become more volatile immediately after the inventory information is released. Not surprisingly, options implied volatility tends to rise and fall in response to this weekly cycle, creating near-term trading opportunities.

Calculating Fair Volatility

Financial markets are driven by individual traders placing real bets with real money. Prices rise when buyers are more aggressive than sellers; they fall when sellers are more aggressive than buyers. When both parties disagree and neither side feels pressured to execute a trade, bid-ask spreads widen. These dynamics alone determine the price of a financial instrument.

The principal goal of an option trader is to arbitrage subtle differences between implied and fair volatility by structuring positions that capitalize on those differences. Perfectly priced options, in which implied volatility accurately represents the behavior of the stock, cannot be used to generate a profit no matter how well structured the position. The underlying stock must rise or fall more or less than the amount priced into some portion of a trade to generate a profit. The shape of the implied volatility surface becomes critical because it allows the various parts of a trade to be priced differently.

Option traders are guided, to a great extent, by historical volatility. However, as we have seen, no single volatility value can be used to explain option prices across different strikes and expirations. The various skews and distortions that make up an implied volatility surface, therefore, reflect the combined opinions of all market participants. These views, and the surfaces they create, are dynamic and unpredictable. In that regard, they tend to invalidate conventional pricing methods built on simple historical volatility of the underlying instrument.

Unfortunately, option prices are very sensitive to volatility. Table 3.2 illustrates this sensitivity by comparing two put series—one with an implied volatility skew and one with flat volatility. The first example (left side) is built around a typical volatility skew; the second (right side) uses the same volatility for all entries. The value selected for the constant volatility side was taken from the at-the-money entry ($145 strike) on the left side of the table.

TABLE 3.2   *Comparison of Skewed and Flat Put Option Series
(Left Side: The skewed version is characterized by rising implied
volatility at lower strikes. Right Side: The flat version uses constant
implied volatility throughout. Calculations are based on a stock price
of $143.49, 1.5% risk-free interest, and 25 days remaining before
expiration.)*

Strike	Volat	Price ($)	Volat	Price ($)
150	0.420	10.10	0.441	10.40
145	0.441	7.34	0.441	7.34
140	0.458	5.11	0.441	4.86
135	0.479	3.47	0.441	2.99
130	0.498	2.27	0.441	1.69
125	0.520	1.46	0.441	0.86
120	0.545	0.92	0.441	0.39

As expected, differences become more dramatic near
the bottom of the table where the implied volatility
skew is steepest. At the $120 strike, a 10% increase in
implied volatility generates a 136% increase in the
option price. Significant differences appear at all levels.
For example, a relatively small (3.8%) difference at the
$135 strike is large enough to generate a 16% increase
in the option price.

We can define volatility as a 1 standard deviation
(StdDev) price change, in percent, at the end of 1 year.
If a stock trades at $100 with a volatility of 40%, then
a 1 standard deviation change in the course of a year
will raise the price to $140 or lower the price to $60.
Using the normal distribution, we can assume a 68%
chance that the final price will fall within this range.
Some adjustment for interest rates is also necessary. If
the risk-free rate of return during this time frame is 5%,
then a 1 standard deviation price change at year end

will be $105 × 40% = $42. We would, therefore, expect the stock to trade between $63 and $147, 68% of the time.

Another key characteristic of volatility is that it is proportional to the square root of time. This dynamic allows us to extrapolate short-term volatility from annual volatility or to project annual volatility from short-term calculations. For example, if a stock exhibits 40% annual volatility, dividing by the square root of the number of weeks in a year will yield a weekly volatility estimate: 0.40 / SQRT(52) = 5.5%. Likewise, because there are 252 trading days in a single year, we can estimate that the same stock will exhibit daily volatility equal to 0.40 / SQRT(252) = 2.5%. For a stock trading at $100, this value simplifies to $2.50 (2.5% the price of the stock). It is also the value of a 1 standard deviation daily price change.

Surprisingly, most traders take a simple view of historical volatility. The most common approach involves calculating a single value based on one month of price changes. For consistency, it is common to use 20 close-to-close values. Historical volatility is calculated as the standard deviation of the short-term returns multiplied by the square root of the number of trading days in a year—also known as the annualization factor. As we saw earlier, this value is equal to SQRT(252) = 15.87. Each return is equal to the natural logarithm of the second close divided by the first: ln(close2 / close1). A sample calculation is illustrated in Table 3.3.

TABLE 3.3   *Historical Volatility Calculations for Amgen (Ticker: AMGN)*

Date	Close	Log Chng.	StdDev	Annual Vol.
2009/04/17	47.07			
2009/04/20	45.74	-0.0287		
2009/04/21	46.09	0.0076		
2009/04/22	45.11	-0.0215		
2009/04/23	46.82	0.0372		
2009/04/24	49.83	0.0623		
2009/04/27	50.18	0.0070		
2009/04/28	50.44	0.0052		
2009/04/29	51.03	0.0116		
2009/04/30	48.47	-0.0515		
2009/05/01	48.61	0.0029		
2009/05/04	48.51	-0.0021		
2009/05/05	47.99	-0.0108		
2009/05/06	47.63	-0.0075		
2009/05/07	47.08	-0.0116		
2009/05/08	47.20	0.0025		
2009/05/11	47.92	0.0151		
2009/05/12	48.22	0.0062		
2009/05/13	48.05	-0.0035		
2009/05/14	48.18	0.0027		
2009/05/15	48.16	-0.0004	0.0230	36.5%
2009/05/18	49.34	0.0242	0.0224	35.6%
2009/05/19	49.94	0.0121	0.0225	35.7%
2009/05/20	50.59	0.0129	0.0217	34.5%
2009/05/21	49.49	-0.0220	0.0213	33.7%

The table includes 5 successive calculations, each based on the previous 20 price changes. It is important to note that volatility varies over the 5 days chosen from a high of 36.5% to a low of 33.7%. This variability further complicates the task of estimating fair implied volatility.

Calculating historical volatility using a month of close-to-close price changes is a reasonable approach when the goal is to structure trades that will remain in place for days or weeks. However, when trading in shorter time frames such as a single day, close-to-close changes are too granular because they merge together intraday, overnight, and weekend information. Unfortunately, this approach has been the standard since options first began trading on an exchange. We can improve on this approach by separately calculating historical volatility in each of these time frames and comparing different stocks with regard to overnight and intraday volatility.

Suppose, for example, that two stocks with similarly priced options have significantly different profiles with regard to intraday and overnight volatility. One stock might exhibit frequent large opening price spikes followed by relative intraday stability, whereas the other might tend to open unchanged before becoming volatile. The first reacts to overnight events around the world; the second reacts to news events that occur during the trading day. The first stock might be a candidate for overnight long straddles initiated near the closing bell; the second might be a candidate for the same trade placed after the market stabilizes around 10:00 in the morning.

We can extend this thinking to differentially calculate volatility for different time frames using different annualization factors. Most significant are the two intervals that make up a trading day: the intraday interval that begins at 9:30 when the market opens and ends at 16:00 when the market closes (O-C), and the overnight time frame from the close at 16:00 to the open at 9:30 (C-O). The intraday interval is 6.5 hours, and the overnight interval is 17.5 hours.

Annualization factors are calculated as shown here:

Intraday

Length (hours)	6.5
Time frames per day	24 / 6.5 = 3.6923
Time frames per year	252 × 3.6923 = 930.4596
Annualization factor	SQRT(930.4596) = 30.5034

Overnight

Length (hours)	17.5
Time frames per day	24 / 17.5 = 1.3714
Time frames per year	252 × 1.3714 = 345.5928
Annualization factor	SQRT(345.5928) = 18.5901

Using these parameters, intraday volatility can be calculated as the standard deviation of the 20 most recent open-to-close price changes multiplied by 30.5. Likewise, overnight volatility is given by the standard deviation of the 20 most recent close-to-open price changes multiplied by 18.6. This approach compensates for reduced intervals with larger annualization factors. As before, the number of days used for the calculation can vary. The number 20 was chosen for consistency. The three key annualization factors are listed in Table 3.4.

TABLE 3.4   *Annualization Factors for Different Time Frames*

Interval	Time Frame	Factor
Daily	Close-to-close	15.87
Intraday	Open-to-close	30.50
Overnight	Close-to-open	18.59

The calculations reveal that the intraday factor is nearly twice as large as the close-to-close factor. As a result, stocks that typically display small overnight price changes will have relatively high intraday volatility. Historical volatility for these stocks is understated because it takes into account a 17.5-hour overnight interval when the stock is not trading, but ignores the magnitude of the intraday swings. In that regard, traditional calculations assume that price changes are evenly distributed over all 24 hours of the trading day. Table 3.5 displays three different volatility calculations for a 21-day time frame (20 daily price changes) for AutoZone. The calculations terminate on 2009/06/03 with the stock trading at $158.80.

TABLE 3.5   *Three Different Historical Volatility Calculations for AutoZone (Ticker: AZO)—(C-C) Denotes Close-to-Close, (C-O) Denotes Close-to-Open, (O-C) Denotes Open-to-Close (Standard deviations and annualized volatilities are listed at the bottom of the chart.)*

Date	Open	Close	Log Chng. (C-C)	Log Chng. (C-O)	Log Chng. (O-C)
2009/05/05	162.60	161.57			
2009/05/06	164.49	163.30	0.0107	0.0179	-0.0073
2009/05/07	164.75	163.02	-0.0017	0.0088	-0.0106
2009/05/08	163.92	157.47	-0.0346	0.0055	-0.0401
2009/05/11	157.26	158.99	0.0096	-0.0013	0.0109
2009/05/12	158.51	156.98	-0.0127	-0.0030	-0.0097
2009/05/13	156.20	154.48	-0.0161	-0.0050	-0.0111
2009/05/14	154.48	156.67	0.0141	0.0000	0.0141
2009/05/15	156.29	158.01	0.0085	-0.0024	0.0109
2009/05/18	158.94	158.71	0.0044	0.0059	-0.0014
2009/05/19	158.20	161.28	0.0161	-0.0032	0.0193
2009/05/20	162.30	157.10	-0.0263	0.0063	-0.0326
2009/05/21	157.45	154.54	-0.0164	0.0022	-0.0187
2009/05/22	154.99	155.65	0.0072	0.0029	0.0042
2009/05/26	156.02	162.84	0.0452	0.0024	0.0428
2009/05/27	159.92	155.04	-0.0491	-0.0181	-0.0310
2009/05/28	155.37	150.56	-0.0293	0.0021	-0.0314
2009/05/29	150.88	152.15	0.0105	0.0021	0.0084
2009/06/01	153.88	156.83	0.0303	0.0113	0.0190
2009/06/02	156.99	158.32	0.0095	0.0010	0.0084
2009/06/03	157.32	158.80	0.0030	-0.0063	0.0094

(C-C) StdDev	0.02272		(C-C) Volatility	36.1%
(C-O) StdDev	0.00739		(C-O) Volatility	13.7%
(O-C) StdDev	0.02114		(O-C) Volatility	64.5%

Properly adjusted historical volatilities using the annualization factors of Table 3.4 are displayed at the bottom of the table. The results are striking. Annual volatility rises to 64.5% when calculated using intraday price changes. Conversely, overnight volatility is just 13.7%. As expected, traditionally calculated daily volatility was a compromise between the two at 36.1%. This number was close to the actual trading value for at-the-money options which calculated as 32% for both June puts and June calls. Implied volatility averaged 35% for all June options, including both puts and calls.

Differential volatility has significant implications because it creates trading opportunities. Table 3.5 revealed that, for AutoZone, intraday price changes are dramatically more volatile than overnight changes. Options are, therefore, underpriced during the day and overpriced when the market is closed. These differences hint at possible day trades. An investor who purchases a straddle at the market open would pay 32% for a position that will exhibit 64% implied volatility for the remainder of the trading day. Conversely, if the position is held overnight, it will be exposed to dramatically reduced volatility (13.7%) and excessive time decay.

These distortions are the rule, not the exception. Table 3.6 lists overnight, intraday, traditional close-to-close, and 252-day volatility for a randomly selected list of optionable stocks. The calculation for 252-day volatility was based on all price changes in a 252-day window.

TABLE 3.6   *Four Different Measures of Volatility for a Randomly Chosen Group of 15 Stocks on 2009/06/03—Overnight (C-O), Intraday (O-C), Daily (C-C), and 252-Day (Column #7 displays the ratio between intraday and overnight volatility. The final column lists at-the-money implied volatility on 2009/06/03.[3])*

Symbol	06/03 Close	Onite Vol.	Intraday Vol.	Daily Vol.	252-Day	Intraday/ Onite	ATM Implied
BAX	49.28	0.08	0.56	0.27	0.35	7.46	0.37
PNRA	52.86	0.17	0.83	0.36	0.58	4.95	0.39
AAPL	140.95	0.13	0.63	0.40	0.58	4.83	0.39
IBM	106.49	0.10	0.46	0.26	0.40	4.67	0.26
AMZN	85.68	0.18	0.81	0.41	0.69	4.39	0.42
NKE	58.17	0.18	0.72	0.41	0.55	4.07	0.36
GS	142.15	0.21	0.84	0.47	0.91	3.95	0.42
ISRG	156.61	0.21	0.83	0.49	0.73	3.90	0.54
MMM	59.50	0.14	0.50	0.34	0.43	3.44	0.29
FDX	56.30	0.24	0.75	0.48	0.60	3.19	0.60
RIMM	80.48	0.25	0.77	0.48	0.82	3.09	0.73
GOOG	431.65	0.14	0.42	0.23	0.52	3.07	0.27
DGX	53.53	0.12	0.38	0.21	0.39	3.06	0.26
DB	65.15	0.56	0.89	0.71	1.05	1.60	0.57
BP	50.75	0.33	0.40	0.38	0.57	1.20	0.33

Two entries near the bottom of the table, Deutsche Bank (ticker: DB) and BP (ticker: BP), have headquarters outside the United States and trade heavily on other exchanges. Deutsche Bank is located in Frankfurt, Germany; BP, a major energy company, is located in London. Each is characterized by a relatively small, although significant, discrepancy between intraday and overnight volatility. Conversely, the top entry, Baxter International Healthcare (ticker: BAX), displays an enormous discrepancy of 7.5x with 56% intraday volatility and only 8% overnight.

In most cases, at-the-money implied volatility closely mirrors the close-to-close calculation listed in the daily volatility column. The 252-day column tends to display higher values because it includes the September 2008–March 2009 time frame, when the market experienced a tremendous drawdown and was relatively unstable. In some cases, at-the-money implied volatility closely mirrors the 252-day number. FedEx (ticker: FDX) is an excellent example where both implied and 252-day values are 60% while the more traditional close-to-close number is only 48%. In such cases, the market anticipates increased volatility and larger price changes and votes with higher option prices. It is important to note that none of the stocks listed had an upcoming scheduled event such as quarterly earnings.

Parsing Price Changes by Weekday

When a stock with high intraday volatility is identified, it would be helpful to know if calendar effects cause one particular day to be superior to another for structuring long positions. We can directly compare price changes between different stocks at different prices by recasting each price change in standard deviations.

Recall that we can divide the annual volatility of a stock by the square root of the number of time frames in one year to determine the volatility for a single time frame. Working in the other direction, we can calculate the standard deviation of the recent price changes and multiply by the stock price to determine the value in dollars and cents of a 1 standard deviation price change. Dividing the next change by this number yields the value of the change in standard deviations.

Extending this method facilitates the recasting of close-to-close, close-to-open, and open-to-close changes in standard deviations. Table 3.7 displays a sample calculation for three open-to-close price changes.

TABLE 3.7   *Calculating Intraday (Open-to-Close) Price Spikes in Standard Deviations (Results are shown in boldface type in column #7. The final column, Calculation, is included for clarity.)*

Open	Close	Log Chng. (C-C)	StdDev Log Chng. (C-C)	1 StdDev (C-C)	(O-C) Price Change	(O-C) Spike	Calculation
184.02	185.19						
186.34	189.43	0.0226					
188.00	185.64	-0.0202					
184.79	181.61	-0.0219					
180.51	185.64	0.0219					
184.34	180.81	-0.0264					
181.49	173.26	-0.0427					
171.64	172.37	-0.0052					
171.30	176.84	0.0256					
178.10	181.43	0.0256					
181.12	178.75	-0.0149					
178.55	180.90	0.0120					
179.35	175.27	-0.0316					
174.74	173.16	-0.0121					
172.37	173.25	0.0005					
174.61	177.39	0.0236					
174.07	168.26	-0.0528					
166.51	170.09	0.0108					
170.19	167.44	-0.0157					
164.23	174.68	0.0423					
175.20	168.18	-0.0379	0.0269	4.52			
169.59	170.12	0.0115	0.0264	4.49	0.53	**0.12**	0.53 / 4.52
170.20	168.19	-0.0114	0.0262	4.41	-2.01	**-0.45**	-2.01 / 4.49
169.20	173.50	0.0311	0.0271	4.69	4.30	**0.98**	4.30 / 4.41

The steps can be retraced by reading across the table:

1. Calculate the log of each close-to-close price change (column #3)

2. Calculate the standard deviation of the logs of 20 price changes (column #4)

3. Multiply each standard deviation value by the daily closing price to determine the value of a 1 StdDev change (column #5)

4. Calculate the value of each open-to-close price change (column #6)

5. Divide each open-to-close price change by the previous day's value of a 1 StdDev spike (column #7) to determine the number of standard deviations represented by the intraday (O-C) change.

It is relatively straightforward to re-create this spreadsheet for overnight (close-to-open) and daily (close-to-close) price changes. In each case, the value of a 1 standard deviation price change is determined using the previous 20 close-to-close price changes—that is, the change being evaluated does not affect its own calculation. Using these methods, we can compute overnight (C-O), intraday (O-C), and daily (C-C) price changes for an individual stock or index. Moreover, applying Excel's weekday function, and sorting the data based on this information, allows us to create a chart comparing average price changes for each day of the week. For the purpose of this analysis, we are interested in comparing the magnitude, not the direction, of each day's price change. The chart is, therefore, constructed using absolute values.

Figure 3.3 displays this information for 1 year (252 days) of Apple Computer stock (ticker: AAPL). Each set of bars displays average price spike information for all three time frames—24-hour, overnight, and intraday—for a specific day of the week.

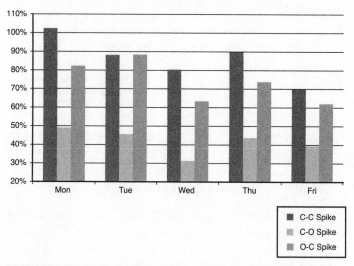

FIGURE 3.3 *Daily (C-C), overnight (C-O), and intraday (O-C) price change summaries by weekday for Apple Computer (ticker: AAPL). Weekday is listed on the x-axis, average price spike in standard deviations on the y-axis. Absolute values are used so that the magnitude, not the direction, is represented. Data spans the time frame from 2008/06/04 to 2009/06/03.*

The chart reveals that close-to-open price spikes (center bar) are not exaggerated by weekends. However, the average close-to-close spike is largest from Friday to Monday. Friday is the calmest day. Day trades that depend on a price spike are least likely to generate profit on this day. Note that it is theoretically possible for the intraday price spike to be larger than the complete close-to-close change on any given day. This behavior occurs after an overnight price reversal. Suppose, for example, that a stock closes at $50, falls to $48 overnight, and rises to $55 the following day. Under these circumstances, the intraday price change would be $7 ($48–$55), but the complete close-to-close change would be only $5 ($50–$55). Differences between close-to-close and intraday bars can be used to infer when this situation occurs with high frequency. If the two bars are close in size, or the intraday bar is larger, then it can be assumed that intraday price changes have a tendency to reverse the direction taken overnight. Likewise, a large difference between the first (C-C) and third (O-C) bars indicates an additive effect where the overnight change tends to reinforce the following intraday move. Figure 3.3 reveals a tendency for Apple stock to experience some reversal between the Monday–Tuesday overnight change and the Tuesday intraday change. As a result, the average close-to-close price spike between Monday and Tuesday is 0.88 StdDev, whereas the average intraday change on Tuesday is 0.89 StdDev. Tuesday represents the largest distortion, and the best opportunity for day trading, because the stock moves as much during the 6.5 hours that the market is open as it does during the 24 hours between the Monday and Tuesday closes. Table 3.6 lists intraday volatility as 63% and daily volatility as 40% for Apple. Based on Figure 3.3, we can further conclude that Tuesday enhances this distortion more than the other days. In real trading terms, Tuesday is the day when the stock is most likely to open lower and close higher, or open higher and close lower.

Investors can create this analysis for a specific stock by downloading prices into a spreadsheet and replicating the process outlined in Table 3.7. The process is repeated for each type of price change, results are averaged, and a small table is constructed containing the results. Figure 3.3 was included for clarity. The underlying data appears in Table 3.8.

TABLE 3.8   *Underlying Data for Figure 3.3*

Weekday	(C-C) Spike	(C-O) Spike	(O-C) Spike
Mon	1.03	0.49	0.83
Tue	0.88	0.45	0.89
Wed	0.80	0.32	0.64
Thu	0.91	0.44	0.74
Fri	0.70	0.39	0.63

Although the analysis should always be focused on individual stocks, the behavior of the overall market can form an important reference. Figure 3.4 illustrates by representing the distribution of price changes for the S&P 500 during the same time frame as that of Figure 3.3.

The S&P 500, as represented by the SPDR exchange traded fund, displayed a remarkably similar pattern to that of Apple Computer stock. Tuesday was the flattest day in terms of the relationship between close-to-close and intraday price changes. As before, this pattern reveals that Tuesday was characterized by the largest distortion with intraday (O-C) price changes rising nearly to the level of the complete close-to-close (C-C) change. As before, the change from Friday to the close on Monday was the largest of the week with the intraday change still disproportionately large. However, Monday and Wednesday were slightly less distorted than the other days because the ratio between 24-hour (C-C) and intraday (O-C) price changes was slightly larger. Once again, Friday was the calmest day with an average close-to-close change of only 0.7 StdDev.

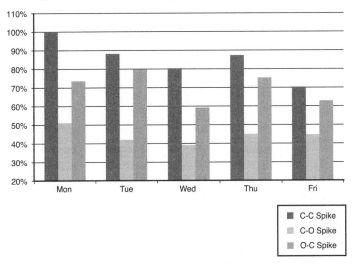

FIGURE 3.4 *Daily (C-C), overnight (C-O), and intraday (O-C) price change summaries by weekday for the SPDR Trust exchange traded fund (ticker: SPY). Weekday is listed on the x-axis, average price spike in standard deviations on the y-axis. Absolute values are used so that the magnitude, not the direction, is represented. Data spans the time frame from 2008/06/04 to 2009/06/03.*

Overall, the data reveals significant, but slightly smaller, distortions in the overall market than in the case of a single heavily traded stock like Apple Computer. In either case, the differences are small relative to what might be expected if traditional option pricing models were valid. For the overall market, across all days, the average 24-hour price change is only

1.2 times as large as the average 6.5-hour intraday change. Of all the distortions in the options market, this is clearly the largest. Extending this analysis to shorter time frames, such as 1 hour or 30 minutes, reveals even larger distortions in which brief price changes can be as large as—sometimes larger than—the 24-hour change. This statement can hold true whether the metric is standard deviations or absolute price change.

In the next section we will explore trading dynamics that capitalize on these volatility distortions.

Trading Volatility Distortions

Because predicting brief price changes in the range of hours or minutes is difficult at best, the most sensible approach is to structure positions early in the day and hold them until they are profitable or the market closes. The goal is to avoid owning dramatically overpriced options during the long overnight time frame when time decay dominates and volatility is diminished. In this regard it is important to note that each week contains 168 hours in total, but only 32.5 trading hours. These can be thought of as low- and high-quality hours. Unfortunately, low-quality hours take their toll as option contracts experience constant time decay that accelerates as expiration approaches.

These dynamics might be interpreted as a reason to sell options and profit from time decay. Many strategies have emerged around these thoughts. Sometimes they can be very profitable. Unfortunately, they require being short options through the turbulent intraday time frame when actual volatility can be several times larger than implied volatility. Worse still, occasional large overnight price spikes can easily erase accumulated profits when the market is closed and the trade cannot be closed. Strategies that involve opening and closing short positions at strategic times—before and after weekends, for example—are flawed because bid-ask spreads often erase most, if not all, of the profit. The market also responds to impending time decay with downward adjustments to option prices. This effect can be seen as declining implied volatility and widening bid-ask spreads near the close on Friday before the long 65.5-hour intervening gap to the next trading day. With few exceptions, selling volatility and time decay is a risky business. One of the most significant exceptions is expiration week, when time decay accelerates and each overnight interval represents a major portion of the remaining time.

Another problem with selling time decay is that profits can only be earned slowly and market exposure is continuous. Conversely, long positions designed to profit from a large price change can generate profit quickly but can only lose money very slowly.

The simplest direction-neutral trade is a long straddle or strangle. A straddle consists of puts and calls at the same strike; a strangle is constructed with different strikes. It is easy to see that a straddle can generate a profit from a large underlying price change in either direction. For example, if we were to purchase a $50 straddle on a $50 stock in which the put and call each cost $2, and the stock price climbed to $70, the call would be worth $20 and the put would be worthless. The overall trade value would, therefore, rise from $4 to $20, yielding a 400% profit.

Such extreme cases are certainly not required to generate a positive return from a long straddle or strangle. Either trade will generate a profit when a large move of the underlying stock causes an imbalance in the deltas, and one side rises in price faster than the other falls. In the extreme case just mentioned, the call side will achieve a delta of 1.00 and the put side will fall to zero. In most situations where the price change is much more modest, the deltas become only slightly skewed. A more reasonable scenario might involve an underlying price change of $4.00 that moves the call and put deltas from a neutral point of 0.44 and -0.44 respectively to 0.65 and -0.25, and the option prices from $5.20(call):$6.00(put) to $9.25(call):$3.20(put). The combined trade value would then rise from $11.20 to $12.45.

Either position, straddle or strangle, should be structured so that the overall trade is delta neutral. The exact center point will vary from day to day depending on implied volatility and time remaining before expiration. However, a delta-neutral position can always be structured at any stock price by adjusting the number of puts and calls. Generally speaking, strangles tend to be a better choice than straddles because the trades are less expensive and the percent gain will always be larger for any size underlying price change.

Our goal is to structure strangles with underpriced options on stocks that tend to exhibit higher volatility than the amount priced into our trade. This goal is best accomplished by selecting stocks with very high intraday to overnight volatility ratios and avoiding long-term trades in which time decay begins to dominate. Especially damaging are trades that span weekends—the most destructive being the final weekend before options expiration.

The best way to assess the viability of this approach for a particular stock is to measure the frequency of large price spikes during open trading sessions. The first step is to create the spreadsheet shown in Table 3.7 for an extended period such as 1 year. As before, absolute values are calculated for all price changes so that the magnitude of the change, not the direction, is recorded. The next step is to select a cutoff value that occurs often enough to make the trade worth placing, and to determine the profit that would be obtained if the stock moved at least that much.

Table 3.9 displays intraday price spike detail for two stocks, Panera Bread (ticker: PNRA) and Intuitive Surgical (ticker: ISRG), listed in Table 3.6.

TABLE 3.9   *One-Year Intraday Price Spike Count for Panera Bread (Ticker: PNRA) and Intuitive Surgical (Ticker: ISRG) (Spikes measured in standard deviations are counted in size categories. Data spans the 1-year time frame from 2008/06/04 to 2009/06/03.)*

Stock	1.5–2.0 StdDev	2.1–2.5 StdDev	2.6–3.0 StdDev	3.1–3.5 StdDev	3.6–4.0 StdDev
PNRA	19	7	3	2	0
ISRG	19	6	8	1	1

The data reveals a large number of intraday price spikes larger than 1.5 standard deviations for both stocks. The profitability of each category for each stock can be determined by simulating the price changes outlined in Table 3.9 and plugging the values into an options calculator that uses the Black-Scholes formula. For PNRA we will select a long strangle composed of $55 calls and $50 puts with 15 days remaining before expiration. The delta-neutral midpoint for this trade is $52.26, which is close to the final trading price listed in Table 3.6.[4] The value of a 1-day 1 standard deviation price change is calculated as follows:

Implied Vol. 39% × $52.26 / 15.87 = $1.28

For ISRG we will select a strangle composed of $155 calls and $150 puts—also with 15 days remaining before expiration. The exact delta-neutral point for this trade is $151.48. Once again, we can calculate the value of a 1-day 1 standard deviation change using the implied volatility listed in Table 3.6:

Implied Vol. 54% × $ 151.48/ 15.87 = $5.15

Intraday trades were simulated by increasing the stock prices in 0.5 StdDev increments from 1.5 StdDev to 3.0 StdDev. Positions were modeled with 15 days remaining before expiration.[5] In each case the trade was opened at 9:30 and closed at 16:00. Results are displayed in Table 3.10.

TABLE 3.10   *Simulated Returns on 1 Strike Wide Strangles for Two Stocks in Different Price and Volatility Ranges—PNRA and ISRG (Positions were initiated with 15 days remaining before expiration at 9:30, and closed at 16:00 [open-to-close]. Calculations are based on 0.25% risk-free interest.)*

PNRA ($)	Change (StdDev)	$55/$50 Strangle	Gain
52.26	0.0	1.44	
54.18	1.5	1.71	18.8%
54.82	2.0	1.92	33.3%
55.46	2.5	2.20	52.8%
56.10	3.0	2.52	75.0%

ISRG ($)	Change (StdDev)	$155/$150 Strangle	Gain
151.48	0.0	11.20	
159.21	1.5	12.43	10.9%
161.78	2.0	13.43	19.9%
164.36	2.5	14.69	31.2%
166.93	3.0	16.17	44.3%

The percentage gains for ISRG can be improved by widening the strike spacing to $10. The delta-neutral midpoint for the new trade, a $155/$145 strangle, is $148.92. Using the same implied volatility of 54% yields a value of $5.07 for a 1-day 1 standard deviation price change. Table 3.11 lists the new values.

TABLE 3.11   *Simulated Returns on 2 Strike Wide Strangles for ISRG ($10 Strike Spacing) (Trades were initiated with 15 days remaining before expiration at 9:30, and closed at 16:00 [open-to-close]. Calculations are based on 0.25% risk-free interest.)*

ISRG ($)	Change (StdDev)	$155/$145 Strangle	Gain
148.92	0.0	8.92	
156.53	1.5	10.09	13.1%
159.06	2.0	11.05	23.8%
161.60	2.5	12.25	37.3%
164.13	3.0	13.66	53.1%

These trades deliver outstanding intraday returns with reasonable frequency. Table 3.9 reveals that each stock exhibited 19 intraday price spikes between 1.5 and 2.0 standard deviations during the 1-year time frame measured. Actual average size across the entire range was 2.1 StdDev for PNRA and 2.2 StdDev for ISRG. Using these values, we can conservatively estimate 31 returns averaging 33% for PNRA, and 35 averaging 24% for ISRG (the 2 StdDev lines in Tables 3.10 and 3.11). Consistently placing intraday trades on both stocks could, therefore, be expected to generate 66 returns averaging 28.2% over the course of a single year. These gains would be partly offset by transaction costs and bid-ask spreads, but in traditional trading terms the risks are very limited.

It is possible that we can enhance the performance of the strategy by incorporating a single overnight time frame—that is, open the trade at 9:30 and close it the following day at 16:00. If evenings near expiration and weekends are avoided, time decay will be minimal. Additionally, actual trading dynamics often support this approach. The sequence of events usually involves insiders and other investors trading on a rumor that is confirmed after the market closes. The stock becomes volatile and rises or falls during the intraday session. If the surprise news reinforces the rumor, the trend will continue into the next day. Because rumors are often wrong, and insiders sometimes have limited or faulty information, the stock often reverses and the trend of the first day is broken. However, because the only risk is a small amount of overnight time decay, it sometimes makes sense to keep the trade open. The decision should be based on the magnitude of the profit achieved during the first day. Generally speaking, "chipping" away at the market and repeatedly capturing small profits is almost always a superior approach. Conversely, attempting to outperform the other market participants by keeping a trade open and forgoing modest profits is a flawed approach because it requires predicting both the direction and the price.

To complete the analysis it is essential to know the frequency of large 2-day open-to-close price spikes. The first step is to repeat the process of creating Table 3.9 using the longer time frame. It is important to note that the value of a 1 StdDev 2-day price change is not twice as large as a 1-day 1 StdDev change. The difference is apparent in the respective annualization factors that convert 1- or 2-day StdDev values into annual volatility. As discussed before, the conversion factor for 1 day is equal to SQRT(252), or 15.87. For a 2-day change the value falls to SQRT(126), or 11.22. We can use the ratio between these two numbers (1.414) as a conversion factor to estimate the value of a 2-day 1 StdDev price change. This number is exactly equal to SQRT(2) because the first time frame is twice as long as the second. Therefore, multiplying the value of a 1-day 1 StdDev price change by 1.4 yields the value of a 2-day 1 StdDev change. Alternatively, we could calculate the precise value by determining the standard deviation of 20 price changes that each span 2 days. Either method is sufficient for this analysis because our goal is to evaluate the feasibility of keeping a trade open overnight to capture a large price change. Appropriate price spike size and frequency information for PNRA and ISRG is presented in Table 3.12.

TABLE 3.12   *Two-Day Price Spike Count for Panera Bread (Ticker: PNRA) and Intuitive Surgical (Ticker: ISRG) (Spikes measured in standard deviations are counted in size categories. Each price change was measured from the open on day 1 to the close on day 2. Data spans the 1-year time frame from 2008/06/04 to 2009/06/03.)*

Stock	1.5–2.0 StdDev	2.1–2.5 StdDev	2.6–3.0 StdDev	3.1–3.5 StdDev	3.5–4.0 StdDev	>4.5 StdDev
PNRA	25	7	1	2	1	0
ISRG	27	4	3	2	3	2

Note: ISRG had 1 spike = 4.83 StdDev and 1 spike = 6.18 StdDev.

Surprisingly, the chart reveals increases in both the size and the frequency of spikes. ISRG experienced 5 price changes larger than 3.5 StdDev across 2 trading days, 2 of which were larger than 4.5 StdDev. At the low end of the spectrum, the two stocks experienced 25 and 27 relatively large spikes in the range of 1.5–2.0 StdDev. In many ways, this number is more significant than the first because it raises the profit frequency to approximately twice each month. Overall, the average change across the entire range was 2.0 StdDev for PNRA and 2.3 StdDev for ISRG. The large number attests to the importance of the intraday time frame because price spikes were measured from the open on day 1 to the close on day 2, while the underlying metric was based on 2 complete close-to-close time frames. This method, in effect, biases the numbers downward as price changes are measured across 2 intraday and 1 overnight session (30.5 hours) while being compared to the size of a 1 StdDev change across 48 hours. Despite the bias, the two stocks averaged 38.5 price changes larger than 1.5 StdDev—a frequency of 15.3%.[6] This value is close to that predicted by the normal distribution, which assumes that 1.5 StdDev price changes occur 13.4 % of the time. The difference between traditional option pricing models and reality grows much larger at the extremes. For example, ISRG exhibited 5 changes larger than 3.5 StdDev—a frequency of 2% or approximately 50 times the theoretical prediction (traditional models set the probability of a 3.5 StdDev change at 0.047%). Moreover, 2 of these changes were larger than 4.5 StdDev—a threshold to which the normal distribution assigns a vanishingly small probability of 0.00068%.

The next step involves repeating the analysis of Table 3.10 using the value of a 2-day 1 StdDev change for each stock. Repeating the previous calculation with the lengthened time frame yields the following implied volatilities:

PNRA: Implied Vol. 39% × $52.26 / 11.22 = $1.82

ISRG: Implied Vol. 54% × $ 148.92 / 11.22 = $7.17

As before, we can use an options calculator to model a series of positions that simulate the price changes displayed in Table 3.12. Once again, positions were initiated with 15 days remaining before expiration; however, in the present case they are opened on day 1 at 9:30 and closed on day 2 at 16:00. In terms of precise option pricing, each trade has 15.60 days remaining before expiration when it is initiated, and 14.33 days left when it is closed at the end of the second day. Results are listed in Table 3.13.

TABLE 3.13   *Simulated Returns on 2-Day Strangles for PNRA and ISRG (Positions were initiated with 15 days remaining before expiration at 9:30 and closed the following day at 16:00. Calculations are based on 0.25% risk-free interest.)*

PNRA ($)	Change (StdDev)	$55/$50 Strangle	Gain
52.26	0.0	1.44	
54.99	1.5	1.90	31.8%
55.90	2.0	2.33	61.5%
56.81	2.5	2.86	98.1%
57.72	3.0	3.48	140.7%

ISRG ($)	Change (StdDev)	$155/$145 Strangle	Gain
148.92	0.0	8.92	
159.68	1.5	10.95	22.7%
163.26	2.0	12.82	43.7%
166.85	2.5	15.10	69.3%
170.43	3.0	17.71	98.5%

Recall that PNRA exhibited 36 price changes averaging 2.0 StdDev, and ISRG exhibited 41 price changes averaging 2.3 StdDev. Combined, the two stocks averaged 2.16 StdDev over 77 price changes. Table 3.13 reveals that a 2 StdDev price change yielded a 61.5% profit for the PNRA option trade, and 43.7% for the ISRG position. These gains are quite substantial considering that the combined frequency exceeds 6 events per month, and the only downside is a small amount of time decay, trading costs, and bid-ask spreads. Unlike many other trading strategies, large profits are generated by disruptive events that move the market in either direction. That said, down is better than up because a falling market (or stock) is always characterized by rising options implied volatility. It is not uncommon to realize a large profit on the put side and no loss on the call side if the market becomes unstable and volatilities rise suddenly. In rare circumstances both sides can generate a profit. This anomaly occurs when the market falls suddenly, implied volatilities rise, and an individual stock stays stable or falls only very slightly. If the price decline is compensated for by rising implied volatility, the call side of a strangle can remain stable while the put side generates substantial profit. In a falling market, the put side profits from both the movement of the stock and rising implied volatility. This asymmetry creates an edge for investors who successfully choose poorly performing or high-risk stocks.

Alternate Trade Structures—Backspreads

Other trade structures can also be used to leverage underpriced volatility. Optimally, the trade should be capable of generating substantial amounts of profit in a short time frame with minimal downside risk. For the two examples we have been following, PNRA and ISRG, a reasonable price change threshold is 2 StdDev. As we have seen, several price changes of this magnitude can be expected each month, with the majority of each change occurring during the intraday session. Long straddles fit the profile of a viable structure because they can generate large amounts of profit from a 2 StdDev price change with only the risk of modest time decay in the event that the stock price remains stable.

Ratio backspreads (reverse ratios) composed of short options at a near strike and a larger quantity of long options at a far strike represent another excellent alternative. An investor who anticipates a large upward price change for a $97 stock might, for example, create a position consisting of 10 short $100 calls and 20 long $105 calls. If the position is delta neutral, small price changes will have little effect. However, a sharp rise in the stock price will generate a profit as the delta of the far strike grows faster than that of the near strike. This trade structure can be thought of as the inverse of the more common forward ratio—in this case 10 long $100 calls and 20 short $105 calls. Forward ratios are designed to generate profit from slow movement and time decay. As such, they are most often held until expiration. For the $100/$105 case, maximum profit is achieved at expiration with the stock trading at $105. In this perfect scenario, the long $100 calls will be worth $5.00 and the short $105 calls will be worth $0.00.

Unfortunately, perfect scenarios rarely occur and forward ratios often lose large amounts of money very quickly. Worse still, the scenario that loses the most money is precisely the one that the original trade was based on—namely, a rise in the stock price. Success depends on an orderly market in which price changes follow the normal distribution and option pricing theory works. As we have seen, those assumptions are misguided, and random large price spikes occur much more often than the models predict. In summary, forward call ratios that are long the near strike and short the far strike fail under the following circumstances:

- The stock rises beyond the break-even point by expiration.[7]

- The stock rises a modest amount early in the life cycle of the trade.

- Market conditions cause implied volatility to rise for all strikes.

- Positive news causes a shift in the shape of the implied volatility skew, and the far strike becomes relatively more expensive.

- The stock falls sharply and both sides of the trade become worthless—excess premium paid for the position is lost. (Most forward ratios are debit trades where the short side only partially covers the cost of the long side.)

- The stock falls sharply but recovers. Implied volatility rises across all strikes and remains relatively high after the recovery causing the far strike to become disproportionately expensive. This effect is very common during periods of market instability as investors shift from one sector to another searching for solid investments. Small sector-specific rallies can occur on rising volatility.

Backspreads (reverse ratios) are profitable under each of these circumstances. They generate profit if the stock rises too far or too quickly, or if implied volatility rises. Furthermore, because the trade is generally sold for a net credit, a sharp move of the stock away from the intended direction results in a small profit—especially if the trade is held until expiration. Forward ratios can only make money slowly but lose it quickly; reverse ratios can make money quickly but only lose it slowly.

These characteristics are perfect for the type of very short-term trading described in these pages. Table 3.14 describes the results of a test constructed around ISRG using the same initial trading price ($148.92), implied volatility (54%), time frame (day 1 at 9:30–day 2 at 16:00), and days remaining before expiration (15). The test explores four different scenarios in which the underlying price rises or falls 1.5 or 2.0 StdDev. For completeness, the table includes an entry showing the maximum loss that can be realized over the brief time frame of the trade.

TABLE 3.14   *Simulated Returns on a 2-Day Backspread (Reverse Ratio) for ISRG (The position being evaluated consists of 10 short $155 calls/20 long $165 calls. The trade is initiated at 9:30 with 15 days remaining before expiration and closed the following day at 16:00. Calculations are based on 0.25% risk-free interest.)*

Description	Short Stock	Long Call ($)	Pos. Call ($)	Net Value ($)	Delta	P&L
Initial trade	148.92	4.16	1.70	-760	0.007	
1.5 StdDev up	159.68	9.32	4.59	-140	0.171	620.00
1.5 StdDev down	138.17	1.13	0.33	-470	-0.045	290.00
2.0 StdDev up	163.26	11.71	6.17	630	0.259	1390.00
2.0 StdDev down	134.58	0.67	0.17	-330	-0.038	430.00
Max loss	149.85	4.26	1.69	-880	0.001	-120.00

Calculating the percent return for a ratio trade is more complex than for a straddle because part of the trade is uncovered and, therefore, has a collateral requirement. Positions are considered covered only if the account is also long options on the same security with more favorable terms—that is, the same or further expiration and closer strike. The standard rule for short equity and index option positions is that the account must have cash or cash equivalent investments equal to 20% of the value of the underlying security minus the amount, if any, that the option is out-of-the-money. A minimum of 10% of the value of the underlying security is used for calls that are far out-of-the-money. For puts the minimum is calculated as 10% of the exercise price. Both short puts and short calls require an additional amount equal to the proceeds from the sale of the option contracts. A position consisting of 10 short $100 calls on a $100 stock would have a collateral requirement equal to:

$0.20 \times \$100$ per share $\times 10$ contracts $\times 100$ shares per contract
$= \$20,000$

Because 10 contracts represent 1,000 shares, it is sometimes easier to think of the calculation as:

$0.20 \times \$100$ per share $\times 1,000$ shares $= \$20,000$

If the stock were initially trading for $98, the correction factor would be:

$(\$100 - \$98) \times 1,000$ shares $= \$2,000$

Subtracting the correction yields a collateral requirement of $18,000 plus the proceeds realized from the sale of the contracts. If the options were priced at $1.30, the collateral requirement would rise by $1,300 to $19,300.

Collateral requirements are reduced, but not eliminated, when long options with less favorable terms can be used to cap losses on the short side. In our example, the 10 short $155 calls have a maximum loss that is capped by the first 10 long $165 calls. The calculation is greatly simplified because the loss is capped at $10 per contract:

($165 - $155) × 1,000 shares = $10,000

Once again we must add the proceeds from the short sale:

$10,000 + $4,160 = $14,160

The account must also have sufficient funds to purchase the long side of the trade (20 long $165 calls equivalent to 2,000 shares of stock):

$1.70 × 2,000 shares = $3,400

Adding together both sides yields the total amount of capital required to place the trade:

$3,400 + $14,160 = $17,560

This number is an accurate representation of the amount of capital put to work for the trade outlined in Table 3.14.[8] The gain or loss cannot be calculated without this number because it represents the true cost. Additionally, the combination of short and long options complicates the situation because the initial position is sold for a $759 credit—that is, the initial trade is short $759. If the position is ultimately unwound for a net cost of $0.00 with both sides having the same value, the profit would be $759. Many investors mistakenly believe that this situation represents a 100% profit because the full amount of the proceeds from the original sale are retained. However, the actual profit is equal to $759 / $17,560 or 4.3% of the total capital consumed. The difference is significant because every account has a limit, imposed by collateral requirements, that determines the maximum obtainable profit.

Based on collateral requirements, we can extend Table 3.14 with percent profit values. Details appear in Table 3.15.

TABLE 3.15   *Simulated Returns, Calculated as a Percentage of Utilized Capital, on a 2-Day Backspread (Reverse Ratio) for ISRG (The position being evaluated consists of 10 short $155 calls/20 long $165 calls. The trade is initiated at 9:30 with 15 days remaining before expiration and closed the following day at 16:00. Calculations are based on 0.25% risk-free interest.)*

Description	Short Stock	Long Call ($)	Pos. Call ($)	Net Value ($)	Delta	P&L ($)	P&L (%)
Initial trade	148.92	4.16	1.70	-760	0.007		
1.5 StdDev up	159.68	9.32	4.59	-140	0.171	620	3.5%
1.5 StdDev down	138.17	1.13	0.33	-470	-0.045	290	1.7%
2.0 StdDev up	163.26	11.71	6.17	630	0.259	1390	7.9%
2.0 StdDev down	134.58	0.67	0.17	-330	-0.038	430	2.4%
Max loss	149.85	4.26	1.69	-880	0.001	-120	-0.7%

Although originally intended as a short-term trade, the lack of time decay risk allows this position to be kept open, without penalty, for an extended length of time. Asymmetry is the trade-off as significant profit can be generated in only one direction if the trade is held until expiration. Maximum profit in the other direction is limited to the initial credit of the trade. That said, because the trade was initially established for a credit, $760 would be realized as profit if the position were to expire with both sides out-of-the-money. Stated differently, if the stock falls or remains at its original price, the position can be allowed to expire worthless for a 4.3% profit. Part of that gain can be realized in the short term if the price falls sharply and both sides lose most of their value. That dynamic is apparent in line 5 of the table, which displays the results of a 2.0 StdDev downward spike. The equivalent upward spike generated a much larger profit of 7.9% because the deltas became imbalanced, causing the far strike to gain value faster than the near strike. After the price change, call and put deltas were 0.705 and -0.482, respectively. Because the long side is twice as large as the short side, the net delta is equal to 0.705 - (0.482 × 2). It is always beneficial to close such trades, keep the profit, and start again.

The final entry in the table displays the maximum loss that can occur at the end of the second day. The small loss is caused by a slight difference in the time decay suffered by the two sides. Because the long side is twice as large as the short side, it experiences slightly more time decay. However, as mentioned before, if both strikes remain out-of-the-money and the trade collapses to zero, the initial credit will be realized as profit. These dynamics create a very low-risk situation and add a level of flexibility that long straddles do not have. Had the stock climbed slightly higher or fallen, the small loss would have vanished. Moreover, keeping the trade open for another day would likely have erased the loss. Strangles behave differently because they suffer from constant time decay.

In summary, short time frames and modest price changes form an excellent environment for long strangles. If, however, the stock price remains unchanged and the position is held until expiration, a strangle will lose 100% of its value. Conversely, backspreads generate smaller profits from modest price changes but are more resilient and can be held without the risk of time decay. A backspread that is held until expiration can generate a reasonable profit with the stock price unchanged. This characteristic makes the trade a better long-term candidate.

Backspreads can also substitute for straddles or strangles in unusual situations in which pricing issues and trading dynamics make these positions difficult to manage. Many excellent examples of this phenomenon occurred during September–October 2008 when U.S. financial markets fell into disarray as the banking system inched toward possible collapse. Goldman Sachs, for example, fell from $170 in early September to $90 in late October. Despite the huge price changes, excessively high implied volatility rendered long straddles nearly worthless as a speculative trading structure. As volatility soared beyond 150%, the time decay cost of an at-the-money straddle exceeded $1.30 per day or $1,300 for a relatively small 10-contract straddle. Unfortunately, the collapse also included calm days when the stock barely moved. These days can be very difficult for an investor paying $1.30 per day to hold a long straddle. Backspreads are a more logical choice for this trading environment.

The September–October 2008 time frame also included very large daily price reversals, some exceeding

25%. Worse still, intraday price reversals as large as 15% were not uncommon. During the two months, there were 22 intraday price reversals larger than 10% and 2 as large as 30%. The overall average intraday reversal, measured as daily (high-low)/close, was 11.3%—a shockingly large number. All structured positions are difficult to manage in this trading environment, which emphasizes the importance of promptly closing profitable trades. The logistics of that discipline are complex because it is difficult, at best, to correctly predict the bottom or top of a trend. Under these circumstances, it is easy to prematurely exit a trade with only a small profit, or to continue holding the trade and become the victim of a sharp reversal. Many investors follow a simple rule: Whenever possible, they close enough of the profitable part of a trade to pay for its initial cost. This approach is reasonable because it allows the investor to continue holding the trade for free. However, reversals still result in lost profit and there is no evidence that this approach yields larger overall returns.

Chapter 4, "Working with Intraday Price Spike Charts," will introduce a new method of technical analysis that can help predict the end of a large intraday price change. Although it cannot be used to predict the direction of the next trend, the ability to capture an interim top or bottom of a large price spike can be a tremendous advantage. The information can be used to time entry and exit points for all or part of a trade or simply to avoid trading during a period of rapid volatile price change.

Volatility and Price Spike Distribution

As we have seen, many stocks exhibit significant differences between intraday, overnight, and daily volatility. This analysis can be extended to determine whether a particular volatility range is best suited for long straddles and backspreads. If, for example, the frequency of large price changes is disproportionately high in stocks that also exhibit high volatility, then these stocks would be preferred targets for straddles, backspreads, or any trade that depends on large price changes. The next step would then be to select intraday trading candidates from this group using more subtle criteria, such as differences between overnight and intraday volatility.

Counting price spikes and parsing according to historical volatility yields the results shown in Table 3.16. Historical volatility for each stock was calculated using the standard deviation of 252 close-to-close price changes.

TABLE 3.16 *Average Number of Spikes Greater Than 2 StdDev and 3 StdDev Sorted by Historical Volatility for 1,771 Optionable Stocks over $20 (Data spans the 1-year time frame from 2008/06/11 to 2009/06/10.)*

Volatility	Avg Spikes > 2 StdDev	Avg Spikes > 3 StdDev
>100	17.55	4.20
91–100	17.36	3.66
81–90	17.29	4.40
71–80	17.23	4.24
61–70	17.66	4.24
51–60	17.57	4.40
41–50	17.82	4.00
31–40	18.28	4.67
21–30	19.30	5.00
0–20	17.65	5.00

The data does not reveal a significant link between volatility and the probability of a large price spike. Because changes are measured in standard deviations, stocks with higher volatility values exhibit proportionally larger price spikes in absolute dollar terms. These differences are anticipated by traditional option pricing methodologies and, therefore, are reflected in option prices.

These results simplify the selection process by removing the requirement to further sort stocks by their historical volatility and shifting the focus to distortions between overnight, intraday, and daily volatility. However, it is important to remember that the analysis is time specific because it depends on market conditions. In previous years, most notably 2007, the percentage chance of a large spike was twice as high for stocks with more than 70% implied volatility as it was for stocks in the lower ranges. This mispricing combined with intraday/overnight distortions created the perfect environment for long straddles, the best candidates being stocks with high implied volatility. It therefore makes sense to occasionally repeat the analysis to determine whether options are generally mispriced with regard to risk in a particular volatility range.

Summary

Implied volatility surfaces are three-dimensional representations that map implied volatility against strike price and expiration date. These maps can be used to spot trading opportunities in the form of subtle pricing anomalies. Institutional traders often consult a library of implied volatility surfaces to locate the most accurate fit for a specific set of market conditions. Volatility can also be mispriced with regard to time of day. It is not unusual for intraday (open-to-close) volatility to be many times larger than overnight (close-to-open) or daily (close-to-close) volatility. As a result, options are often underpriced during the intraday trading session because their prices are based on close-to-close calculations that span the overnight interval. This distortion can be exploited using trade structures that benefit from a large price spike in either direction.

Endnotes

1. VIX options settle on the Wednesday that is 30 days prior to the third Friday of the calendar month immediately following the expiring month. This timing formula causes VIX options to settle on the Wednesday preceding equity options expiration 8 times, and the Wednesday following equity options expiration 4 times each year. The settlement value is based on a special opening quotation of the VIX calculated from the sequence of opening prices of the options used to calculate the index on the settlement date.

2. Equity and index options expire on Saturday at 23:59 following the third Friday of each month.

3. For each of the listed stocks, the differences between put and call implied volatilities were less than 1%. Values were calculated using 0.25% risk-free interest with the target range for the federal funds rate set at 0.00% to 0.25%.

4. The exact delta neutral midpoint for the trade was determined using the Black-Scholes formula.

5. For precision, calculations assumed 15.60 days remaining at the open and 15.33 at the close. Equity and index options expire on the Saturday following the third Friday of each month at 23:59.

6. Because days can overlap, the number is not reduced by half in the 2-day analysis. For example, price changes can be measured from day 1 (open) to day 2 (close), or day 2 open to day 3 close, or day 3 open to day 4 close.

7. The break-even point for a 1:2 ratio composed of 10 long $100 calls and 20 short $105 calls is $110 minus the net cost of the original trade. If, for example, the initial trade had a debit of $2.00, the break-even point would fall to $108. At expiration, with the stock trading at $108, the 10 long $100 calls would be worth $8,000 and the 20 short $105 calls would be worth $6,000, yielding a net credit of $2,000 (the original cost of the trade). Higher ratios such as 1:3 have lower break-even points.

8. Collateral and margin requirements for option traders can vary from one broker to another. Furthermore, recent changes allow customers whose accounts exceed certain minimum thresholds to take advantage of portfolio margining rules that more precisely align collateral requirements with overall portfolio risk. Readers wanting to further explore margin and collateral requirements are encouraged to visit the Chicago Board Options Exchange Web site and to contact their brokers.

Chapter 4

Working with Intraday Price Spike Charts

Key Concepts

- Option pricing theory can be extended to measure the volatility of a series of price changes over very brief time frames of just a few minutes. Results can be visualized as a series of bars on a histogram chart.

- These histograms are useful tools for identifying several different types of price change behavior: rising instability that often precedes a large change; decreasing volatility near the end of a sharp up or down trend; and sudden up-down or down-up transitions that sometimes precede changes in direction.

- Although these indicators cannot be used to predict the direction that a stock will ultimately take, they can be used as entry points for certain types of trades, or as triggers for legging into multipart trades. They can also be useful for timing exit points for existing positions.

- The frequency and magnitude of large price changes in very brief time frames is much larger than option pricing theory predicts. These large spikes present unique opportunities to option traders because they are not comprehended in the price.

- Many contemporary trading platforms include tools that allow the creation of price spike charts in real time using minute-by-minute or tick-by-tick information.

Introduction—A New Charting Tool

Volatility often reveals more about the behavior of a stock or index than any other technical parameter. Volatility rises when prices become unstable; when prices become unstable they usually fall. The link between market instability and falling prices is the underlying theme behind the widely followed CBOE Volatility Index (VIX). During the sharp market decline of September–October 2009, the VIX climbed from 20 to a peak above 85. By June, after the Dow climbed from its March low of 6,500 to a new high of 8,700, the VIX had fallen to 30. Rumors, news, and a variety of market events contribute to volatility at all levels, including that of individual stocks.

It is always helpful to study price changes in the context of volatility—that is, they should be measured in standard deviations. For example, a $5.00 change for a $100 stock with 40% historical volatility is much smaller (2 StdDev) than a $3.00 change for a $50 stock with 30% implied volatility (3.2 StdDev).

Most stock charts suffer from a major deficiency in that they don't provide a straightforward way to accurately measure the relative size of each price change. Relatively small price changes are sometimes hidden inside a series of large bars, and large price changes can be disguised by relatively small bars. As always, the phenomenon is related to volatility. In the first case, the distortion is caused by a series of large price changes that translate into high volatility. Seemingly large changes can be relatively small when compared to the other members of the series. Conversely, in the second case, a very large price change—perhaps twice as large as the other members of the series it appears in—can appear small in absolute size. However, if the stock has been calm, and the price changes have been very subtle, a sudden and steady rise in the relative size measured in standard deviations can be very significant.

Traditional charting approaches can also conceal the differences between orderly and disorderly markets. An orderly market can be built on a series of consistent, but large, price changes, whereas a disorderly market is often characterized by a series of small inconsistent changes. The latter can be very confusing if the stock price remains relatively unchanged over an extended period of time while also becoming increasingly unstable. This rising instability may not be visible in a traditional price chart.

The principal goal of an option trader is to arbitrage subtle differences between implied and fair volatility by structuring positions that capitalize on those discrepancies. In that regard, trading options is equivalent to buying and selling standard deviations. Generally speaking, it is important to measure and chart the value that is being traded. Options represent two tradeable parameters: price of the underlying security and volatility measured in standard deviations. Both should be included in any charting strategy.

In a technical charting sense, rising levels of instability often mark the end of a brief but sharp uptrend. This instability can be visualized as increasingly large up and down price spikes. Sometimes they take the form of a single pair of spikes in opposite directions. Conversely, a sharp consistently downward trend often ends with successively smaller downward price spikes followed by a significant upward spike. The final upward spike is often generated by a wave of short covering.

In this chapter we will review a charting strategy that facilitates this type of analysis by recasting minute-by-minute price changes in standard deviations and displaying the results as a histogram at the bottom of a stock chart. One of the most powerful advantages of this approach is its usefulness for comparing stocks that trade at different prices with different underlying volatilities. Our goals will be to use this analysis to spot differential volatility where up and down spikes occur with distinctly different frequency, and to reliably predict the end of an up or down trend. The latter is important to option traders initiating multipart trades with long and short components.

Basic Calculations

Recall that we can estimate annual volatility by calculating the standard deviation of a series of price changes, and multiplying the result by an annualization factor equal to the square root of the number of individual price changes in a single year. As always, each calculation is based on the log of the price change rather than the absolute magnitude. If, for example, the standard deviation of the 20 most recent daily price changes for a $100 stock is 0.158, annual volatility would be equal to:

$$\$100 \times 0.0158 \times SQRT(252) = 25.08\%$$

The calculation can be thought of as consisting of two parts: the determination of the value of a 1-day 1 standard deviation change, and the annualization of that number. The first calculation ($100 × 0.0158) yields the value in dollars and cents of a 1-day 1 standard deviation price change ($1.58). The second multiplies this value by the square root of the number of trading days (15.87) to generate an annual volatility estimate.

The log of each price change is used because option pricing theory assumes that future prices are lognormally distributed. The distinction between lognormal and normal is important. Because a normal distribution is symmetrical, for every possible upward price movement there must be a possibility of an equally large downward price movement. If prices were normally distributed, a $20 stock would have the same probability of rising to $50 as falling to −$10. Clearly this cannot happen. If we assume, however, that price changes are continuously compounded, five 10% upward price changes will raise a $20 stock by $12.21 to $32.21. The corresponding downward price changes would reduce the price by $8.19 to $11.81 because the percent decrease shrinks with each price change. The compounded upward change is 61%, and the corresponding downward change is only −41%. The distribution of final prices is skewed so that no price ever falls below zero. Continuous compounding, therefore, causes future prices to be lognormally distributed. Stated differently, the logs of the price changes are distributed according to the normal distribution curve.

Using a sliding window, we can continuously calculate the value of a 1-day 1 StdDev change—the first part of the calculation—and display these values as a histogram at the bottom of a stock chart. An example is displayed in Figure 4.1.

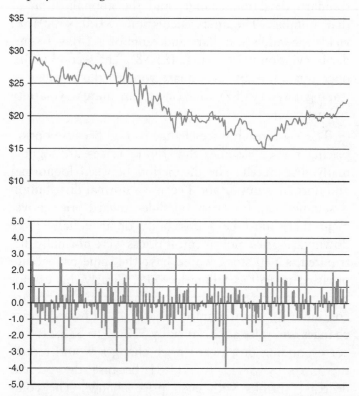

FIGURE 4.1   *Daily closing prices for Microsoft (ticker: MSFT) for 1 year ending on 2009/06/10. The upper pane displays closing prices. The lower pane displays price changes calculated in standard deviations—each change is measured against the standard deviation of the logs of the most recent 20 changes.*

The method for calculating the lower chart is illustrated in Table 4.1.

TABLE 4.1   *Method for Calculating Price Spikes in Standard Deviations (Results to be displayed in a histogram chart are highlighted in boldface type in column D.)*

A Close	B LogChng	C StdDev Log	D Spikes	E Calculation
27.51				
26.87	–0.0235			
25.88	–0.0375			
25.98	0.0039			
26.03	0.0019			
25.85	–0.0069			
25.23	–0.0243			
25.45	0.0087			
25.25	–0.0079			
25.15	–0.0040			
26.15	0.0390			
27.26	0.0416			
27.52	0.0095			
25.86	–0.0622			
25.64	–0.0085			
25.80	0.0062			
26.43	0.0241			
25.44	–0.0382			
26.16	0.0279			
25.50	–0.0256			
26.11	0.0236	0.7084		
26.23	0.0046	0.7008	**0.169**	(26.23 – 26.11) / .7084
25.72	–0.0196	0.6614	**–0.728**	(25.72 – 26.23) / .7008
25.44	–0.0109	0.6564	**–0.423**	(25.44 – 25.72) / .6614
25.28	–0.0063	0.6527	**–0.244**	(25.28 – 25.44) / .6564

The first standard deviation value (column C) appears in row 21 of the table at the end of 20 price changes. The value displayed is equal to the standard deviation of the logs of the 20 most recent price changes (column B) multiplied by the closing price on the current day (26.11). It represents, in dollars and cents, the value of a 1-day 1 StdDev price change. We can extrapolate annual volatility by multiplying this value by the square root of the number of trading days in a year. However, that result is not needed for this analysis. The price spike values displayed in column D are determined by dividing the value of each day's price change by the previous day's value for a 1 StdDev change. For clarity, the calculations are displayed in column E.

It is important to note that each price change is measured against a window that ends just ahead of the change—that is, the change being measured does not influence its own calculation. If the change being measured were part of the calculation, the value would be distorted, and the size of the distortion would be large for short windows. After each calculation, the window is moved forward 1 day and the next price change is measured against the new window. Table 4.1 displays four calculations (boldface type). In this example, 21 closing prices provide data for 20 changes; day 22 is the first to be measured.

This method for displaying daily price changes will be used on a minute-by-minute basis throughout the remainder of this chapter. As might be expected, the dynamics change significantly when the time between closings is reduced from 1 day to 1 minute. Most significantly, the relationship between the value of a 1-day 1 StdDev change and annual volatility does not persist at the single-minute level. As we shall see, it would not be reasonable to estimate annual volatility from a series of single-minute price changes because they are generally much too volatile. This difference is significant because it reveals that short-term changes often represent distortions. Regression toward the mean smoothes these differences over longer time frames, making it possible to price options. In the very short time frame of a few minutes, options can dramatically underprice risk. This distortion can represent a tremendous opportunity when an individual stock experiences a price change that, on an annual basis, would be equivalent to several standard deviations.

The distortion can be visualized in a chart that measures short-term price changes against the implied volatility of a stock. An example of this concept is illustrated in Figure 4.2, which charts a single day of price changes for AutoZone (ticker: AZO) in 2-minute intervals. Price spikes were calculated in standard deviations using implied volatility for at-the-money options (34%) as a reference. Replacing a sliding window of price changes with actual implied volatility allows us to compare the magnitude and frequency of the changes with theoretical predictions derived from option prices.

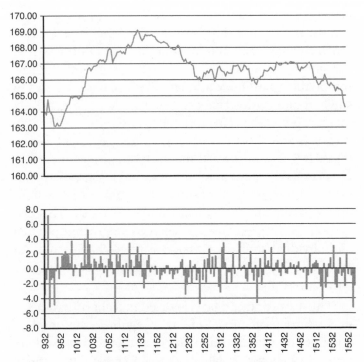

FIGURE 4.2   *Intraday prices for AutoZone on 2009/04/22.*
Changes are displayed in 2-minute intervals. The upper pane displays
closing prices. The lower pane displays price changes calculated in
standard deviations—each change is measured against the implied
volatility of at-the-money options (34%). Time of day is displayed on
the x-axis.

For each 2-minute interval, the value of a 1 StdDev
change was calculated using fixed implied volatility of
34% and the current closing price. A sample calculation
taken from the first 2-minute interval is outlined in the
following sequence of steps:

Implied Volatility 0.34

Closing price $164.45

2-minute intervals per year 252 days × 24 hours × 30 per hour = 181,440

Correction factor SQRT(181,440) = 425.96

2-minute volatility 0.34 / 425.96 = .000798

1 StdDev for 2 minutes .000798 × $164.45 = $0.13

2-minute price change $164.45 – $164.00 = –$0.45

2-minute change in StdDev –$0.45 / $0.13 = –3.46 StdDev

The day was marked by very large price changes and reversals. Despite the appearance of 11 spikes larger than 4 StdDev, the stock closed virtually unchanged (open = 164.45, close = 164.28). The actual distribution of large price changes is listed in Table 4.2.

TABLE 4.2 *Comparison Between Actual and Theoretical Price Spike Frequency for Spikes Larger Than 1 StdDev (Total population was 195 price changes. All are displayed in Figure 4.2.)*

StdDev	Actual Count	Actual Frequency	Predicted Frequency
>7	1	0.5%	2.6E–12
>4	11	5.6%	0.006%
>3	21	10.8%	0.3%
>2	41	21.0%	4.6%
>1	92	47.2%	31.7%

The difference between actual and expected frequency is very large across the entire group. The frequency of all changes larger than 1% was elevated nearly 50% while larger spikes, greater than 3 StdDev, occurred 36 times as often as option pricing theory predicts (a 3 StdDev spike should occur only once in approximately 330 price changes).

Price Spikes at the Single-Minute Level

Because the relationship between annual volatility and individual price changes becomes decoupled in very brief time frames, it is more reasonable to measure each price change against the most recent. This approach also provides a more sensitive and accurate measurement because it takes into account the current environment. For example, if price changes are very modest for an extended period of time, the value of a standard deviation falls, increasing the sensitivity to rising short-term volatility. This measurement is important for detecting the top of an uptrend after the market has experienced a steady orderly series of gradual increases. Conversely, if the reference is fixed using annual volatility, subtle increases will be difficult to detect.

The calculation method shown in Table 4.1 can be replicated in any time frame. Figure 4.3 displays a recalculated version of Figure 4.2 using a 20-price-change window as the reference for each bar in the histogram.

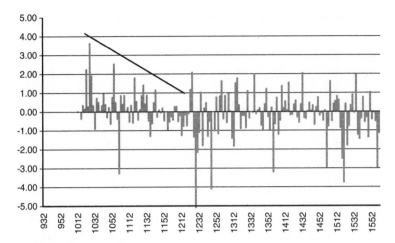

FIGURE 4.3 *Intraday price changes for AutoZone on 2009/04/22 calculated in standard deviations using a sliding window of 20 price changes as the reference.*

The new version appears distinctly different from the lower pane of Figure 4.2, where the reference was implied volatility of at-the-money options. Most notable is the large 5.1 StdDev downward spike at 12:28. This change is significantly smaller and difficult to notice on the original chart because it is measured against a relatively large implied volatility. In Figure 4.3, the metric is the previous 20 price changes, which are quite small and, therefore, increase the sensitivity of the measurement. The difference is important because this spike marks the end of the $5 uptrend.

More significant is the downward sloping line near the left side of the chart that marks successive decreases in the size of the up spikes. This trend is less distinct in the previous figure because it depends on subtle relationships that occur during the brief time frame of the chart. In Figure 4.3 it is also followed by the sharp downward spike mentioned previously. Drawing the line from the bottom of the large downward spike to the top of the first large upward spike steepens the slope, further emphasizing the likely end of the uptrend.

It is also possible to customize the analysis by slightly adjusting the use of the sliding window. The most reasonable modification delays moving the window forward after every second calculation so that each pair of price changes can be measured using the same reference value for a 1 StdDev change. This strategy solves a slight problem that is caused when one large spike diminishes the value of the next by increasing the size of the 1 StdDev reference at the end of the window. Logistically the accommodation is simple. The first and second price changes after the window are simultaneously calculated before the window is shifted. The method is illustrated in Table 4.3.

TABLE 4.3   Alternate Method for Calculating Price Spikes in Standard Deviations (The 20-price-change window is shifted forward only after 2 successive price changes have been calculated. This approach prevents a large price change from diminishing the value of the next.)

	A Close	B LogChng	C 1StdDev	D spike 1	E spike 2
1	37.91				
2	37.90	–0.0003			
3	37.88	–0.0005			
4	37.92	0.0011			
5	37.96	0.0011			
6	37.86	–0.0026			
7	37.86	0.0000			
8	37.87	0.0003			
9	37.86	–0.0003			
10	37.85	–0.0003			
11	37.85	0.0000			
12	37.76	–0.0024			
13	37.81	0.0013			
14	37.76	–0.0013			
15	37.84	0.0021			
16	37.86	0.0005			
17	37.86	0.0000			
18	37.83	–0.0008			
19	37.80	–0.0008			
20	37.86	0.0016			
21	37.84	–0.0005	0.0455		
22	37.82	–0.0005	0.0456	–0.439	
23	37.85	0.0008	0.0461		0.659
24	37.88	0.0008	0.0457	0.651	
25	37.89	0.0003	0.0446		0.217
26	37.88	–0.0003	0.0387	–0.224	

Each pair of price spikes, listed in columns D–E, is measured against the same standard deviation value in column C. In this example the first pair of results, displayed in rows 22–23, are measured against the first standard deviation value in row 21; the second pair in rows 24–25 are measured against the row-23 value; the row-26 result, measured against the row-25 standard deviation value, begins a new pair. These five values can be combined simply by adding together columns D–E to create a series: –0.439, 0.659, 0.651, 0.217, –0.224. As before, the series is plotted directly below the stock chart.

With this approach we can modify the use of the sliding window to accommodate more complex scenarios where it is important to measure several spikes against the same value without having one spike influence the next by its contribution to the calculation. However, extending this approach too far disrupts the analysis, which is designed to measure price changes against the most recent trend—that is, the underlying metric for a large spike increases as large spikes are added to the analysis.

Lengthening the window also decreases the impact of a single large price spike. Conversely, shortening the window too far invalidates the standard deviation calculation. The examples in this book were all calculated using a 20-price-change window. This length is appropriate for studying price-change behavior in time frames that span 20–30 minutes. However, it may be necessary to further shorten the window when studying very brief time frames. Experimentation is always the key. Later in this chapter we will review an example based on tick-by-tick data in which window selection is critical because the number of ticks can vary significantly between stocks and time frames.

Examples of Ultra-Short-Term Volatility Swings

Examples of rising and falling short-term volatility can be found in virtually any stock chart on any day. The following examples are designed to illustrate the link between price-change behavior and volatility.

Example 1

Figure 4.4 displays three significant instances for Intuitive Surgical (ticker: ISRG) that occurred on 2009/06/04. The chart depicts single-minute changes in standard deviations measured against a 20-price-change window. As before, the upper pane displays stock prices and the lower pane displays the price spike diagram. ISRG was chosen for this example because it tends to exhibit frequent very short-term price swings.

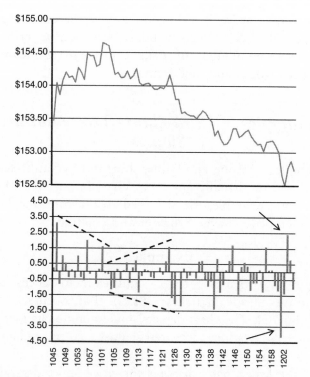

FIGURE 4.4   *Minute-by-minute price-change profile for ISRG on 2009/06/04 between 10:45 and 12:05. The upper pane displays the stock price; the lower pane displays price changes in standard deviations measured against the most recent 20-price-change window. Price and standard deviations are marked on the y-axis of each graph, and time is marked on the x-axis. Dashed lines and arrows mark specific patterns discussed in the text.*

Three major signals appear on this chart. The first signal shows the deterioration of the uptrend beginning at 10:45 (the downward-sloping dashed line near the left side of the lower chart). The second signal is marked by the two dashed lines tracing an increasingly wide path from 11:05 to 11:30. This period is marked by increasing volatility as indicated by a tendency toward larger price spikes in both directions. During most of this interval, prices were relatively stable just above $154. However, the stability interval ended with one large upward spike at 11:24, and three large downward spikes at 11:25, 11:26, and 11:28. Continuing large spikes are significant because each raises the value of a 1 StdDev change by its contribution to the 20-price-change window. After this event, the stock fell quickly for several minutes before reaching the final pair of very large spikes marked by arrows at the right side of the chart. These opposing spikes represent the third signal on the chart. They can be expected to mark an end to the downtrend and, possibly, a reversal. Figure 4.5 allows us to check this prediction by extending the chart an additional 2 hours.

FIGURE 4.5   *Extension to Figure 4.4 for the purpose of checking reversal prediction.*

The prediction of an end to the downtrend is verified by the new upward price change that begins 10 minutes later, at 12:15, and continues until 12:53. The reversal signal would have been a reasonable trigger for launching the short put side of a complex trade, purchasing the long call side of a complex trade, or closing a long put or short call position for a profit.

Example 2

Similar dynamics can be used to predict the beginning of a new trend after a quiet period marked by relatively low volatility. Continuing its volatile behavior, ISRG displayed an excellent example just 1 day after the changes depicted in Figures 4.4 and 4.5. The stock climbed sharply at the open to $169, where it remained for most of the trading day. Prices became unstable after 13:00 and the stock began falling. The moving window price spike chart gave advance indications that the stock was becoming unstable. Relevant charts covering the time frame are displayed in Figure 4.6.

Increasing volatility during the quiet period is marked by a downward-sloping dashed line. The interval of the line ends with a sudden reversal—a 2.1 StdDev upward spike followed by a 1.8 StdDev downward spike. This reversal at the end of a series of successively larger downward spikes signals that the price has become unstable. The result was a rapid $2 decline in the stock price. Once again, the price spike chart reliably predicted an entry/exit point for some or all of a trade. In this regard it is important to stress, once again, that we cannot predict the size or length of the impending transition. However, once the stock begins falling, price spike information can usually be used to predict the end of the decline. This information is particularly valuable when the new trend persists for an extended period and the bottom can be reliably predicted.

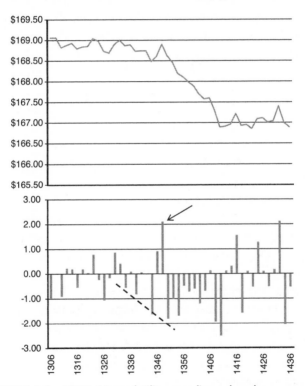

FIGURE 4.6 *ISRG rising volatility preceding a drawdown on 2009/06/11. Price and standard deviations are marked on the y-axis of each graph, and time is marked on the x-axis. Each price change represents a 2-minute interval.*

Example 3

Unusual openings marked by large price swings often provide excellent trading opportunities. Initial downtrends sometimes reverse as bullish investors capture the opportunity to buy stocks at reduced prices. Such reversals are common when the fall of a single stock mirrors a broader market decline rather than news on the stock itself. This behavior can be distinguished from a more serious sell-off that launches a new trend. Figure 4.7 illustrates with a 2-minute price chart of AutoZone on 2009/06/10 immediately after the open. The stock fell rapidly, mirroring a 100-point sell-off of the Dow. However, decreasing volatility marked by a series of successively smaller negative spikes signaled that the downtrend was ending. The decreasing volatility trend is marked with a dashed line near the left side of the chart.

Such events represent excellent opportunities for selling puts or buying calls. New short put positions are especially profitable under these circumstances because they are initiated at higher implied volatility in a falling market with the stock at a low price. When the trend reverses, the short position can be closed at a higher underlying price and reduced implied volatility. In this example, a series of successively smaller downward spikes ended in a reversal to a 1 StdDev upward price change. This reversal marked the best entry point for a short put position.

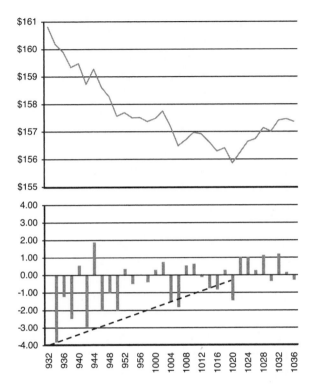

FIGURE 4.7 *Opening downtrend for AutoZone on 2009/06/10. Each price change represents a 2-minute interval. Time is marked on the lower x-axis, price and standard deviations on the y-axis.*

Example 4

Charts that are constructed on single- or multiple-minute boundaries often suffer from distortions related to artificial time boundaries. In trading terms a minute is a long time. Large price changes near the end of a minute can disguise 55 seconds of relatively flat performance; large changes at the beginning can create the false impression of rising volatility. Furthermore, some minutes contain hundreds of individual ticks whereas others contain very few. A more accurate picture is obtained when stock prices are charted as a continuous series of individual ticks.

The lack of artificial time boundaries also enhances the effectiveness of volatility analysis. Figure 4.8 illustrates this concept using a series of bars that are each composed of 10 ticks. During the time frame of the chart, each 10-tick bar spanned approximately 6 seconds—approximately 100 ticks per minute. The chart displays data for Amazon.com (ticker: AMZN) beginning on 2009/06/12 at 14:46 and ending at 15:00. As before, the reference window was 20 price changes long (200 ticks).

Figure 4.8 is characterized by two important features. The first, marked by arrows, is composed of large opposing price spikes that follow a calm period with relatively few price changes. This sharply rising volatility is somewhat asymmetrical as the downward spike is 4.3 StdDev while the upward spike is only 3.1 StdDev. This instability led to a drawdown which lasted several minutes. The second feature, marked by parallel dashed lines visible at the right side of the chart, marks the end of the price decline. This interval is characterized by increasingly large upward spikes and increasingly smaller downward spikes. These characteristics are unlikely to support the continuation of the downtrend, which ends abruptly after the 2.5 StdDev upward spike.

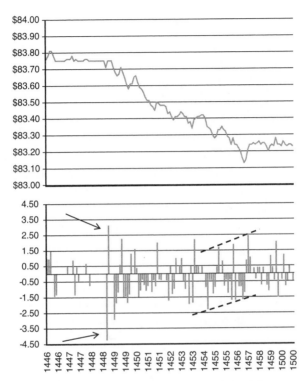

FIGURE 4.8   *Price spikes measured at the tick level for Amazon.com on 2009/06/12 between 14:46 and 15:00. Each bar represents 10 ticks. Arrows mark large opposing price spikes that follow a calm period with relatively few trades and low volatility. Dashed lines near the right side of the chart mark the beginning of a reversal. Time is measured on the x-axis is for reference only as there are no time boundaries in tick-by-tick data.*

Summary

Price-change behavior can be studied using histogram charts that recast changes in standard deviations measured against a moving window of fixed length. The resulting charts can be used to identify rising and falling volatility and make predictions based on the price stability of the underlying security. These predictions can often be used to identify the end of a trend or to predict that a stock is becoming unstable. Traders can use this information to select entry and exit points for complete trades or parts of trades. The latter case is helpful when the goal is to leg in or out of a complex position.

The distortions that appear in these charts persist at the tick level, where the removal of artificial time barriers improves the accuracy of the technique. Fine-tuning of the method involves adjusting the length of the window and the number of ticks per price change.

Chapter 5

Special Events

Key Concepts

- Traditional option pricing is based on the assumption that markets trade continuously. In reality, the market is open for 6.5 hours and closed for 17.5 hours on normal trading days, and closed for 65.5 hours each weekend. The relative magnitude of these distortions increases sharply as expiration approaches.

- The market efficiently responds to these distortions by depressing and inflating option prices in predictable ways. These changes can be used as the basis for highly profitable trades.

- News events often create brief inefficiencies as the market absorbs and responds to new information. These inefficiencies represent outstanding trading opportunities that sometimes persist for several hours.

Introduction

Traditional option-pricing methods are built on the assumptions that markets trade continuously, and that price changes follow the lognormal distribution—a smooth, predictable statistical function. The result has been a set of formulas that predict the fair value of an option based on time remaining before expiration and consistent underlying volatility. These assumptions have been consistently proven wrong, and the market always responds efficiently with adjustments to option prices. The most obvious adjustment, discussed in Chapter 1, "Basic Concepts," is the implied volatility skew or smile. This distortion is designed to guard against out-sized downward spikes that are not comprehended by traditional pricing theory. It causes out-of-the-money puts to be aggressively priced with significantly higher implied volatility than at-the-money options.

Timing causes another major distortion. The market is open for 6.5 hours and closed for 17.5 hours on normal trading days. Friday evening the market closes for 65.5 hours until Monday at 9:30. These distortions become more significant as options expiration approaches. The final weekend of each expiration represents 33% of the time remaining before the contracts expire.[1] More significantly, it represents 39% of the time left before the market closes at 16:00 on Friday and the contracts can no longer be traded. The market responds to these distortions by depressing option prices near the close on Friday and reinflating them on Monday morning. In pricing terms, implied volatility falls near the close on Friday to compensate for impending weekend time decay and rises Monday morning to restore prices to normal levels. This anomaly becomes even more dramatic on expiration Thursday when the overnight time frame between Thursday's close and Friday's open consumes 17.5 of the remaining 24 hours before current-month options stop trading.

Planned high-impact events represent another distorting force that confounds traditional option pricing models. Earnings announcements are an excellent example. Implied volatility often rises sharply before a quarterly earnings announcement to accommodate the perceived risk of a surprise. Stocks with a history of "low-quality" announcements that differ markedly from analyst expectations are most affected. In some cases implied volatility can rise several-fold. After the announcement, regardless of the results, implied volatility falls rapidly as the stock settles at an appropriate new price. These situations are difficult to trade because there is no precise way of knowing whether the preannouncement implied volatility is too low, correct, or too high. Furthermore, put:call parity inflates both sides whereas the market tends to perceive risk as being on either the upside or the downside. This situation causes one of the two sides to be dramatically overpriced regardless of the magnitude of the surprise.

Planned news events can have a similar effect across the entire market. Examples include interest-rate announcements by the Federal Open Market Committee (FOMC) of the Federal Reserve, presidential speeches, congressional votes, OPEC meetings, and a variety of international events such as meetings of central bankers in other countries. Less significant events such as the Weekly Petroleum Status Report, which is issued each Wednesday at 10:30 by the Energy Information Agency (EIA), can also provide trading opportunities because implied volatility tends to rise before the event and fall immediately after. The EIA report is particularly interesting because oil prices tend to spike up or down immediately after the report, establishing a new short-term direction. After prices settle, implied volatility falls and new trading opportunities emerge based on the new trend. Once set in motion, the industry tends to move in the same direction until the next major piece of news, which, in many cases, is the next weekly report.

Properly exploited, these opportunities can form the basis of a trading strategy that involves selectively entering the market on rare occasions to capture large profits in very brief time frames.

Unavoidable Volatility Distortions

Many of these anomalies persist because they represent market efficiencies rather than inefficiencies. An excellent example, related to the beginning of expiration week, occurred while this book was being written. The event, which was mentioned briefly in Chapter 1, materialized when expiration week began on Easter Sunday, causing the market to be closed for an extra day—Good Friday. This extension of the final weekend before expiration caused the market to be closed for 89.5 hours from Thursday at 16:00 to Monday at 9:30. These 89.5 hours represented 47% of the 192 hours left before the final close on expiration Friday. The situation was exacerbated by an unusually calm market on Thursday as many traders, private investors, hedge fund managers, and Wall Street executives left early for a long weekend vacation.

As is always the case in such situations, option buyers were hesitant to overpay for contracts that were guaranteed to suffer enormous time decay before the next trading opportunity on Monday morning. We can verify, using an options calculator, that $100 calls trading with 50% implied volatility on a $100 stock will collapse from $3.19 to $2.47 during this final long weekend.[2]

However, the situation is complex because option sellers must weigh the risks associated with exposure to world events over a long weekend. Anything can happen when the market is closed, and the danger is compounded by the fact that corrective trades cannot be executed. Despite the risk, buyers usually win and prices tend to collapse near the close of the final trading day. Sellers normally offset their risks with a variety of cleverly structured hedges on the broad market that employ long out-of-the-money puts, and short positions on stocks, stock futures, and indexes. The effect is also stock-specific in the sense that securities perceived to have lower risk tend to experience greater option price collapses than riskier stocks—in the April 2009 situation, financial stocks were considered risky but most technology stocks were not.

Research in Motion (ticker: RIMM) was one of many stocks that exhibited persistently falling implied volatility from the open to the close on Thursday, April 9. Specifically, implied volatility for at-the-money options declined steadily from 65% at the open to 50% at the close. This decline was entirely predictable because it exactly offset the weekend time decay so that a return to 65% implied volatility on Monday precisely restored option prices to their closing values on Thursday. Stated differently, investors who purchased RIMM call options as the market closed on Thursday were not penalized for the three-day gap because they paid dramatically reduced prices.

This efficiency of the market represented a tremendous trading opportunity because it condensed three days of time decay near the end of an expiration cycle into a single trading day. A simple structured position consisting of 1 long $60 call and 2 short $65 calls returned more than 80%—the trade cost $0.89 at the open and sold for $1.61 at the close with the stock price nearly unchanged (the stock opened at $63.99 and closed at $64.18—a move of just $0.19). Actual trading prices for the position throughout the day are displayed in Figure 5.1.

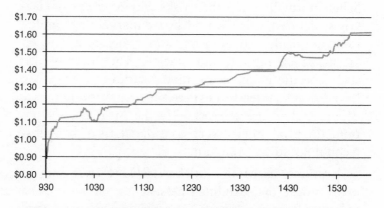

FIGURE 5.1   *Trading price of a 1:2 ratio consisting of 1 long $60 call and 2 short $65 calls for Research in Motion over Easter weekend 2009. The trade returned more than 80% in just 6.5 hours with virtually no change in the underlying stock price.*

Day trading the stock would have been very difficult because precise timing would have been required to capitalize on small intraday price changes. In this regard options are superior trading instruments because they can generate profit from volatility collapse or time decay without any change in the underlying stock price. Furthermore, the option position was hedged against substantial movement of the stock, making it relatively direction neutral.

Day trading the option was simple—it required nothing more than opening a position in the morning and closing it in the afternoon. Moreover, the trade generated a steadily growing profit throughout the day as implied volatility collapse followed a straight path with a steep slope of 2.3% per hour.

Anomalies of this sort are rare but their enormous profit potential cannot be ignored. A very aggressive investor could have opened several such trades over the long Easter weekend and realized the equivalent of a year's worth of successful investing.

Event Trading

Carefully chosen market-moving events present the same sort of opportunity. Although most are not as profitable as the expiration week example, many occur on a regular basis. The weekly Petroleum Status Report issued every Wednesday at 10:30 is an excellent example. It provides tremendous detail regarding inventories of all crude-oil and petroleum products, such as gasoline and distillate fuel oil. The report often contains surprises that cause oil prices and the prices of oil-related stocks to reset to new levels. For example, the May 13, 2009, report revealed that U.S. crude-oil imports averaged only 8.7 million barrels per day, down 1.2 million barrels per day from the previous week. The report also mentioned that crude-oil imports for the previous four weeks had averaged 257,000 barrels per day less than the same four-week period during the previous year. Inventory levels also indicated a slowdown in usage—at 370.6 million barrels they were above the upper boundary of the average range for this time of year. In general terms the report was negative because it seemed to indicate that demand destruction resulting from a weak economy was creating an oversupply.

The market reacted quickly. Both crude-oil prices and oil-company stocks experienced rapid declines that persisted throughout the day. The exchange traded fund OIH, which represents a basket of oil services and exploration companies, is among the most sensitive to the weekly petroleum status report. Figure 5.2 displays 2-minute closing prices and an appropriate price-spike diagram for OIH on 2009/05/13. The peak near the left side of the price chart (upper pane) appeared just after the report was released.

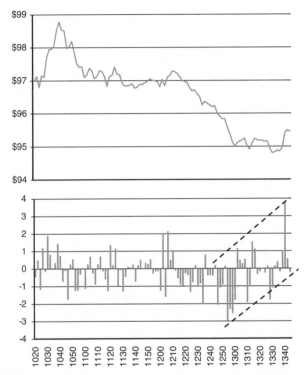

FIGURE 5.2 *OIH closing prices (2-minute) and matching price-spike diagram on 2009/05/13. Time is marked on the x-axis, trading price and standard deviation on the y-axis. The end of the downtrend is marked by two upward sloping parallel lines in the spike chart (dashed lines).*

The situation was optimized for selling current-month call options because it was expiration week and only 2 trading days remained. These dynamics increase the sensitivity of near-the-money options to large price changes. At the peak, the $100 call was worth $1.41. It declined to just $0.35 at the bottom of the downtrend 3 hours later. June options, with 1 month remaining before expiration, were also viable candidates for the trade. The June $100 call declined from $5.40 at the peak to $3.75 at the bottom.

We could also have capitalized on the trade by purchasing May $95 puts, which climbed from $0.58 at the peak to $1.95 at the bottom of the drawdown with the options $0.15 in-the-money. Finally, the corresponding June put climbed from $4.50 to $6.04.

The exit point for the trade is apparent in the price-spike diagram, which, as before, displays price changes in standard deviations. The end of the trend is marked by two upward-sloping parallel lines that indicate successively larger upward spikes and correspondingly lower downward spikes. As is common, the trend is apparent before the stock reverses direction.

Petroleum status reports are unusual because the length and complexity of the information introduces a brief inefficiency into the market as the new information is digested. Once it becomes clear that prices are too high or too low, traders must make decisions about moving billions of dollars. Some of those decisions must necessarily depend on the size and speed of the adjustment. All of this activity takes time because no particular method of technical analysis can predict the news. As illustrated in Figure 5.2, these dynamics create a brief trading opportunity until the market, once again, becomes random. However, this type of trading is certainly not without risk. In many cases the market immediately reacts to a specific item in the report before reversing direction after all the information is analyzed. These reversals can be much more severe than the original trend ignited by the news. This effect is evident in Figure 5.2 because the initial upward spike located near the left side of the chart occurred just after the report was released; the trend immediately reversed, the stock stabilized around $97, and after some delay it began falling. The final downward move began with a brief period of instability visible in the price spike diagram after 12:00.

Reversals can also be confusing when they are caused by short covering. When a large number of traders hold short positions in anticipation of negative news, and the stock falls, profit taking can cause a sharp upward spike. "Short squeezes," as they are commonly known, are very common in event-driven trading situations. On the options side these scenarios normally result in widening bid-ask spreads. It is wise to check the short interest data before trading the results of a major news event.

Summary

This chapter reviewed two distinctly different event-based scenarios. The first represented a pricing distortion related to a long weekend just prior to expiration week. This distortion represents a market efficiency rather than an inefficiency because it involves discounting of prices to accommodate excessive, but inevitable, time decay. The market accommodation essentially packs three days of time at the end of the expiration cycle into a single 6.5-hour trading day.

The second example capitalizes on the market's adjustment to a relatively large amount of new information. The opportunity arises as the market briefly becomes inefficient while digesting the new data.

Many other similar opportunities exist in the complex series of news events and announcements that drive the markets. Each is characterized by a unique set of timing parameters and price distortions that must be understood before the event can be properly traded. These examples were designed as guides to help investors find other profitable scenarios.

Endnotes

1. Equity and index options expire Saturday at 23:59. The last trading opportunity for public customers is Friday at 16:00.

2. This calculation assumes a 0.25% risk-free interest rate.

INDEX

Page numbers followed by *n* indicate topics located in endnotes.